TABLE OF CONTENTS

CW00505667

01

CAR ELEMENTS

They are judiciously placed in the design of the car for an optimal operation and occupying a minimum space at minimum weight.

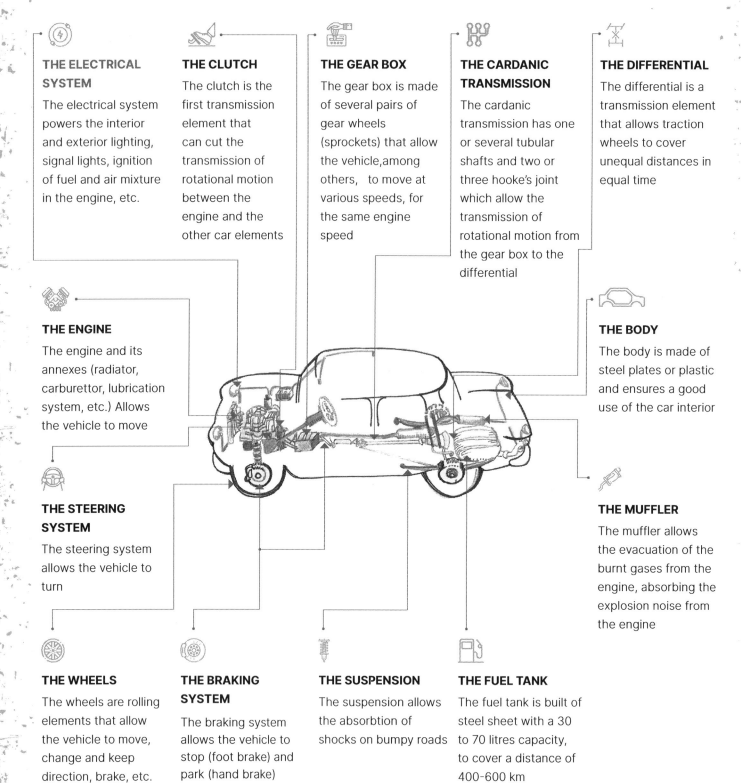

THE ELECTRICAL SYSTEM
The electrical system powers the interior and exterior lighting, signal lights, ignition of fuel and air mixture in the engine, etc.

THE CLUTCH
The clutch is the first transmission element that can cut the transmission of rotational motion between the engine and the other car elements

THE GEAR BOX
The gear box is made of several pairs of gear wheels (sprockets) that allow the vehicle, among others, to move at various speeds, for the same engine speed

THE CARDANIC TRANSMISSION
The cardanic transmission has one or several tubular shafts and two or three hooke's joint which allow the transmission of rotational motion from the gear box to the differential

THE DIFFERENTIAL
The differential is a transmission element that allows traction wheels to cover unequal distances in equal time

THE ENGINE
The engine and its annexes (radiator, carburettor, lubrication system, etc.) Allows the vehicle to move

THE BODY
The body is made of steel plates or plastic and ensures a good use of the car interior

THE STEERING SYSTEM
The steering system allows the vehicle to turn

THE MUFFLER
The muffler allows the evacuation of the burnt gases from the engine, absorbing the explosion noise from the engine

THE WHEELS
The wheels are rolling elements that allow the vehicle to move, change and keep direction, brake, etc.

THE BRAKING SYSTEM
The braking system allows the vehicle to stop (foot brake) and park (hand brake)

THE SUSPENSION
The suspension allows the absorbtion of shocks on bumpy roads

THE FUEL TANK
The fuel tank is built of steel sheet with a 30 to 70 litres capacity, to cover a distance of 400-600 km

The engine is the aggregate that makes the car move.

The engine can be placed:

- At the front of the car
- At the back of the car

THE DRIVE WHEELS (Which receive the rotational motion from the engine) May also be:

- **Rear**
  It is a rear wheel drive vehicle
- **Front**
  It is a front wheel drive vehicle

THE CLASSIC SOLUTION

FRONT ENGINE - REAR WHEEL DRIVE

- Good weight distribution
- Protection of passengers in case of accident
- Short engine and gearbox commands
- Large boot
- Heat at feet level in winter
- Necessity of cardanic transmission
- Reduced interior space and lifted body due to the "tunnel of cardanic transmission"
- Engine generated heat during summer
- Low stability on turns
- Engine exposed to impact

USED BY:

- MOSKVICH
- VOLGA
- FORD
- FIAT 1300
- FIAT 124, 125, ETC.

"FULL FRONT" THE MODERN SOLUTION

FRONT ENGINE AND WHEEL DRIVE

- Low body of the car
- Engine accessibility
- Good wheel drive on difficult
- Ground
- Good weight distribution
- Elimination of cardanic
- Transmission
- Accident protection
- Heat at feet level in winter
- Low cost
- Increased stability when turning
- Construction front axle complications
- Engine exposed to impact
- Reduced ability to climb ramps

USED BY:

- WARTBURG
- TRABANT
- RENAULT16, ETC.

"FULL BACK" THE MODERN SOLUTION

BACK ENGINE AND WHEEL DRIVE

- Low cost
- Low body of car
- Good wheel drive on climbing ramps
- Engine protection on impact
- Uneven weight distribution
- Weak protection of passengers in case of accident
- Engine sucks much dust
- Small boot
- Complicated commands on engine and transmission elements
- Cold at feet level in winter

USED BY:

- FIAT 600 850
- RENAULT 10
- DACIA 1100, ETC.

A CAR ENGINE IS AN INTERNAL COMBUSTION ENGINE

It is named as such because the fuel is burnt inside the engine in a space called ...combustion chamber

This is a scheme of a sectioned engine

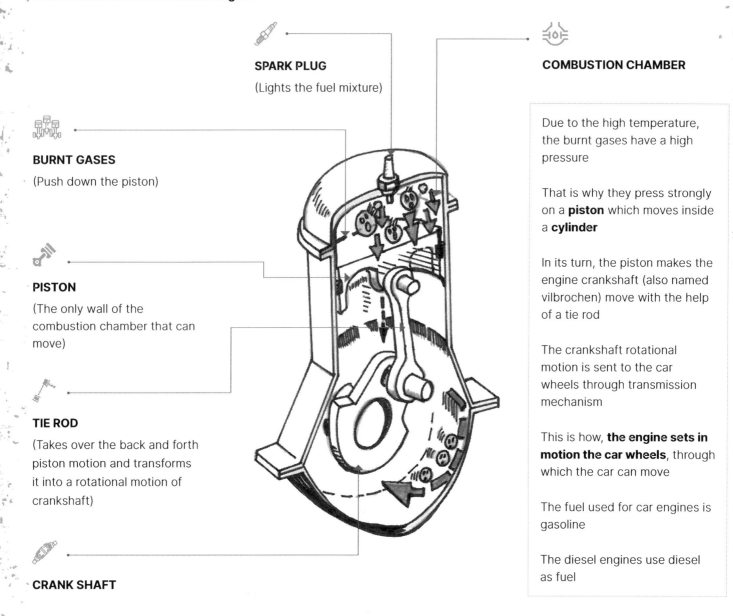

SPARK PLUG

(Lights the fuel mixture)

COMBUSTION CHAMBER

BURNT GASES

(Push down the piston)

PISTON

(The only wall of the combustion chamber that can move)

TIE ROD

(Takes over the back and forth piston motion and transforms it into a rotational motion of crankshaft)

CRANK SHAFT

Due to the high temperature, the burnt gases have a high pressure

That is why they press strongly on a **piston** which moves inside a **cylinder**

In its turn, the piston makes the engine crankshaft (also named vilbrochen) move with the help of a tie rod

The crankshaft rotational motion is sent to the car wheels through transmission mechanism

This is how, **the engine sets in motion the car wheels**, through which the car can move

The fuel used for car engines is gasoline

The diesel engines use diesel as fuel

Unlike the car engine, **the steam locomotive** is an **external combustion**

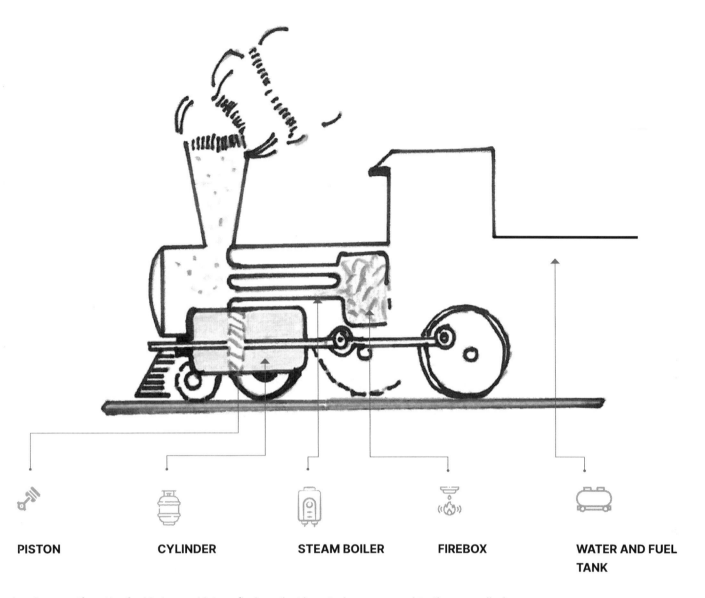

PISTON   **CYLINDER**   **STEAM BOILER**   **FIREBOX**   **WATER AND FUEL TANK**

In a locomotive, the fuel is burned into a firebox that is exterior compared to the car cylinder

As burnt gases are soft they heat the water which turns into steam

The steam is brought into the locomotive engine where it pushes a piston that moves, setting the locomotive wheels into motion

In external burning a small part of the heat produces the locomotive motion, that is why the engine performance in this case is low

At present diesel locomotives are built, having an internal combustion engine, which are strong and have high performance

CARBURETTOR

Gasoline has to mixed with air in order to burn; it is known that air contains oxygen which fuels combustion. **The carburettor** is the element where gasoline is mixed with air, necessary for burning

A basic carburetor **is made of** the following main parts:

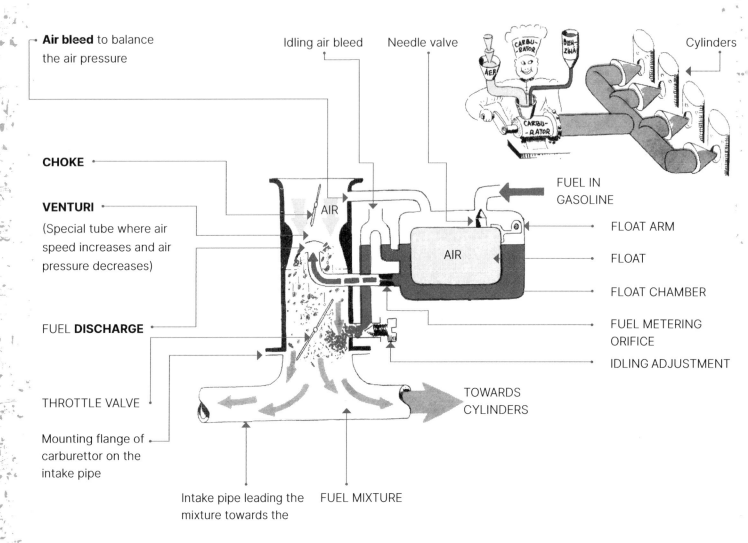

Air bleed to balance the air pressure

Idling air bleed

Needle valve

Cylinders

CHOKE

VENTURI
(Special tube where air speed increases and air pressure decreases)

FUEL **DISCHARGE**

THROTTLE VALVE

Mounting flange of carburettor on the intake pipe

AIR

AIR

FUEL IN GASOLINE

FLOAT ARM

FLOAT

FLOAT CHAMBER

FUEL METERING ORIFICE

IDLING ADJUSTMENT

TOWARDS CYLINDERS

Intake pipe leading the mixture towards the

FUEL MIXTURE

The fuel brought from the tank has a higher pressure than the atmospheric pressure.

Inside the intake pipe the pressure is lower than the atmospheric one, due to the aspiration of piston into the cylinder and to the venturi effect; the air-fuel mixture is absorbed at high speed into the intake pipe and from here into the engine cylinders

The air high speed and low pressure in the venturi make the gasoline move constantly inside the float chamber, through the fuel metering orifice towards the venturi, where it sprays, mixing with air

As soon as the gasoline in the float chamber is consumed, its level decreases, the float lowers and the needle valve opens the orifice through which gasoline comes from the tank

Then the float rises and the needle valve closes again the fuel in orifice. The fuel level will stay constant;

Fuel metering orifice is meant to dose the amount of fuel absorbed into the venturi

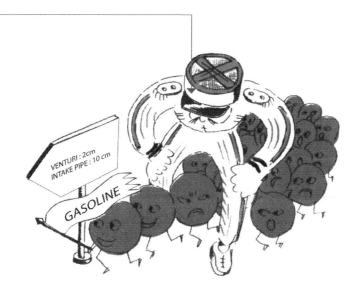

VENTURI : 2cm
INTAKE PIPE : 10 cm

GASOLINE

AIR

AIR-FUEL RATIO

For a normal and complete combustion, it is: -15-20 kg air to 1 kg fuel or -10-12 m3 air to 1 kg fuel

For a larger quantity of air, the mixture is **poor** in fuel and for a smaller quantity of air the mixture is **rich** in fuel

The air quantity is regulated by the choke valve

The throttle valve is controlled by the throttle pedal

When the throttle pedal is pressed, the valve spring is stretched and the valve opens

The mixture passes in high quantity into the intake pipe, feeding the cylinders the crankshaft spins at high **speed**

On **releasing** the pedal, the valve is attracted by the spring and closes the fuel and the air are sucked through a small pipe; the amount of mixture is lowered and the crankshaft spins at low speed. The engine goes at idle speed

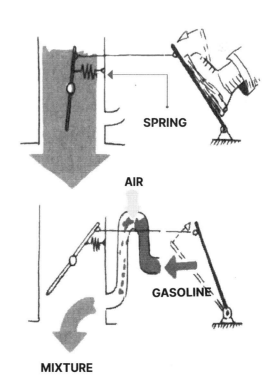

SPRING

AIR

GASOLINE

MIXTURE

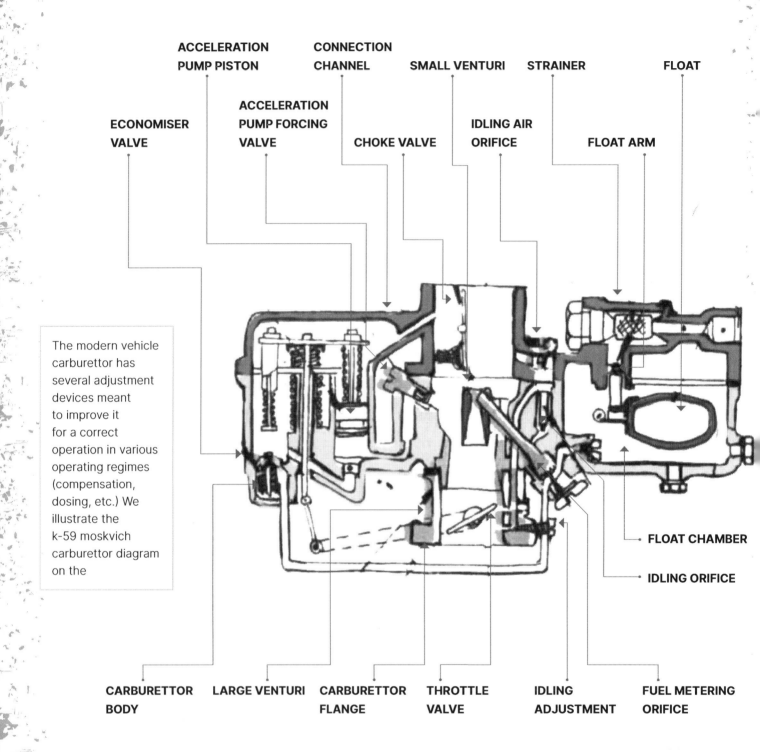

ACCELERATION
PUMP PISTON

CONNECTION
CHANNEL

SMALL VENTURI

STRAINER

FLOAT

ECONOMISER
VALVE

ACCELERATION
PUMP FORCING
VALVE

CHOKE VALVE

IDLING AIR
ORIFICE

FLOAT ARM

The modern vehicle
carburettor has
several adjustment
devices meant
to improve it
for a correct
operation in various
operating regimes
(compensation,
dosing, etc.) We
illustrate the
k-59 moskvich
carburettor diagram
on the

FLOAT CHAMBER

IDLING ORIFICE

CARBURETTOR
BODY

LARGE VENTURI

CARBURETTOR
FLANGE

THROTTLE
VALVE

IDLING
ADJUSTMENT

FUEL METERING
ORIFICE

THE FUEL SUPPLY SYSTEM

The fuel supply system is made of air and fuel elements the air sucked into the carburettor must be clean and have no dust.

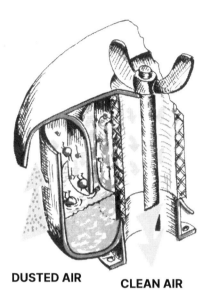

DUSTED AIR　　**CLEAN AIR**

THE AIR FILTER

The air filter is the element that cleans air of dust

The air in the atmosphere enters the filter and close to the oil it changes direction suddenly

As dust is heavier than air, it penetrates oil not being able to follow air on changing direction

The strainer has the role of retaining the dust residues moved by air that have not penetrated oil in certain filters the strainer is sodden in oil for a better effect in air purification

Not using the air filter leads to engine wear in a very short time

The dust in the air is made of very fine but hard particles ; a simple calculation leads to the conclusion that a vehicle which runs 100,000 km on paved roads, sucks into its engine about 300...500 grams of dust. Reaching the parts of the car through friction, the dust makes them wear and shortens the engine lifespan.

On a country road dust is more abundant and the premature wear risk is greater.

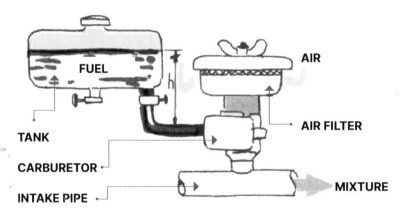

Direct supply: due to the height difference (h), the fuel flows from the tank to the carburettor this is a dropping system; the construction is simple but dangerous because of the possibility to have fires

The gas pump is used to pump the fuel from the tank into the carburettor to the vehicles that do not have the tank above the engine; it has 2 operational stages: aspiration and release.

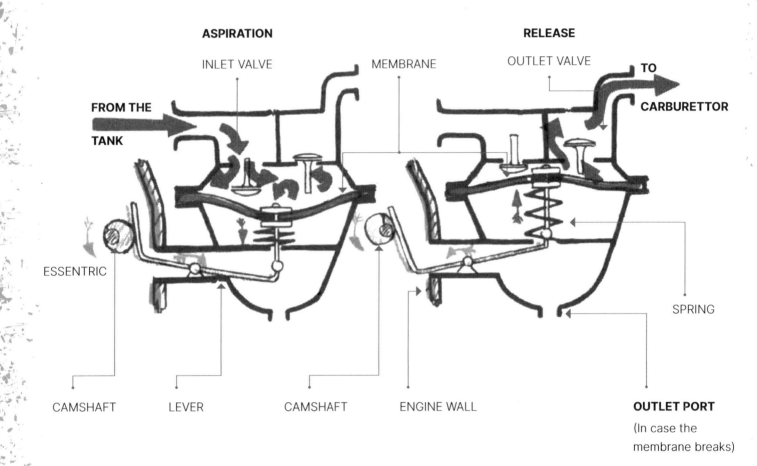

ASPIRATION

INLET VALVE · MEMBRANE

FROM THE TANK

ESSENTRIC

CAMSHAFT · LEVER · CAMSHAFT · ENGINE WALL

RELEASE

OUTLET VALVE

TO CARBURETTOR

SPRING

OUTLET PORT
(In case the membrane breaks)

When the lever is separated from the eccentric shaft, the membrane is lowered, and the spring is compressed; a loss of pressure happens above, opening the inlet valve and the fuel is sucked into the pump

When the lever approaches the eccentric, the membrane is pushed up by the spring ; overpressure is created above, closing the inlet valve and opens the outlet valve; fuel is pumped to the carburettor

FOUR-STROKE ENGINE

For an engine to work, it is necessary that the fuel-air mixture be brought into the cylinder

On opening the inlet valve, the mixture enters the cylinder, being sucked due to depressure created by piston descent.

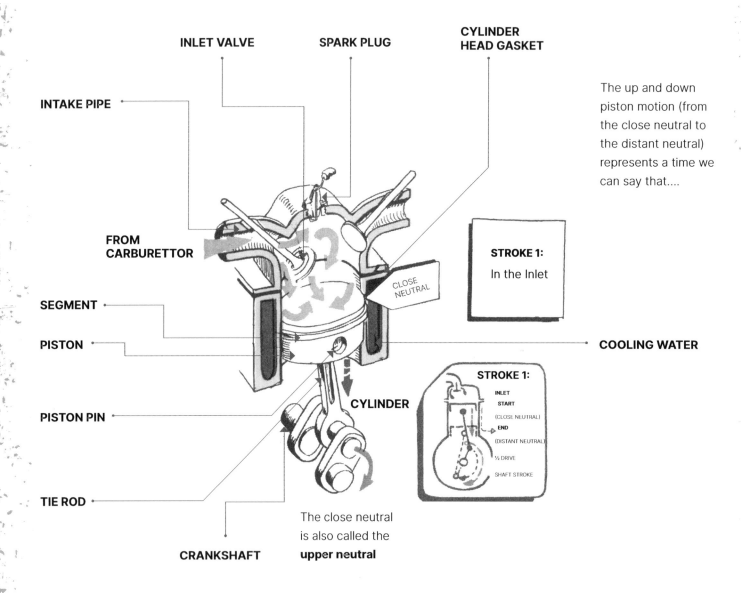

INLET VALVE

SPARK PLUG

CYLINDER
HEAD GASKET

INTAKE PIPE

The up and down
piston motion (from
the close neutral to
the distant neutral)
represents a time we
can say that....

FROM
CARBURETTOR

CLOSE
NEUTRAL

STROKE 1:

In the Inlet

SEGMENT

PISTON

COOLING WATER

PISTON PIN

CYLINDER

STROKE 1:

INLET

START

(CLOSE NEUTRAL)

END

(DISTANT NEUTRAL)

½ DRIVE

SHAFT STROKE

TIE ROD

The close neutral
is also called the
upper neutral

CRANKSHAFT

CYLINDER HEAD **COMBUSTION CHAMBER**

When intake is over the piston reaches the distant neutral (distant limit position from the combustion chamber)

Igniting the mixture in this situation will lead to no result, as the pressure of burnt gases could not push the piston, which is at the end of its way

It is necessary to bring the piston into its initial position, that is into close neutral

The inlet valve closes too, for the mixture not to leave the cylinder

Thus, during the return stroke, the piston compresses the mixture in the cylinder head, named **combustion chamber**

Keeping the "time" term for piston motion, we can say...

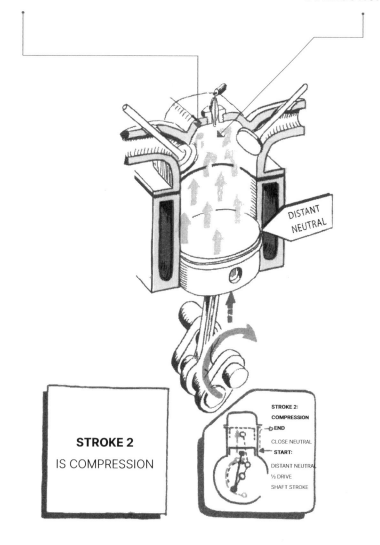

DISTANT NEUTRAL

STROKE 2
IS COMPRESSION

STROKE 2:
COMPRESSION
END
CLOSE NEUTRAL
START:
DISTANT NEUTRAL
½ DRIVE
SHAFT STROKE

The distant neutral is also called the **lower neutral**

SPARK PLUG

At the end of compression the piston is again at the close neutral point

The mixture compressed in the combustion chamber occupies a reduced volume, and has a high pressure (approx. 10 Atm)

The spark plug makes a high voltage spark that lights the fuel-air mixture

The burnt gases that resulted from the burning of fuel in the presence of air have a high temperature and pressure (approx. 35 Atm) making them expand

Under the pressure of burnt gases the piston is pushed towards the distant neutral, spinning the engine crankshaft

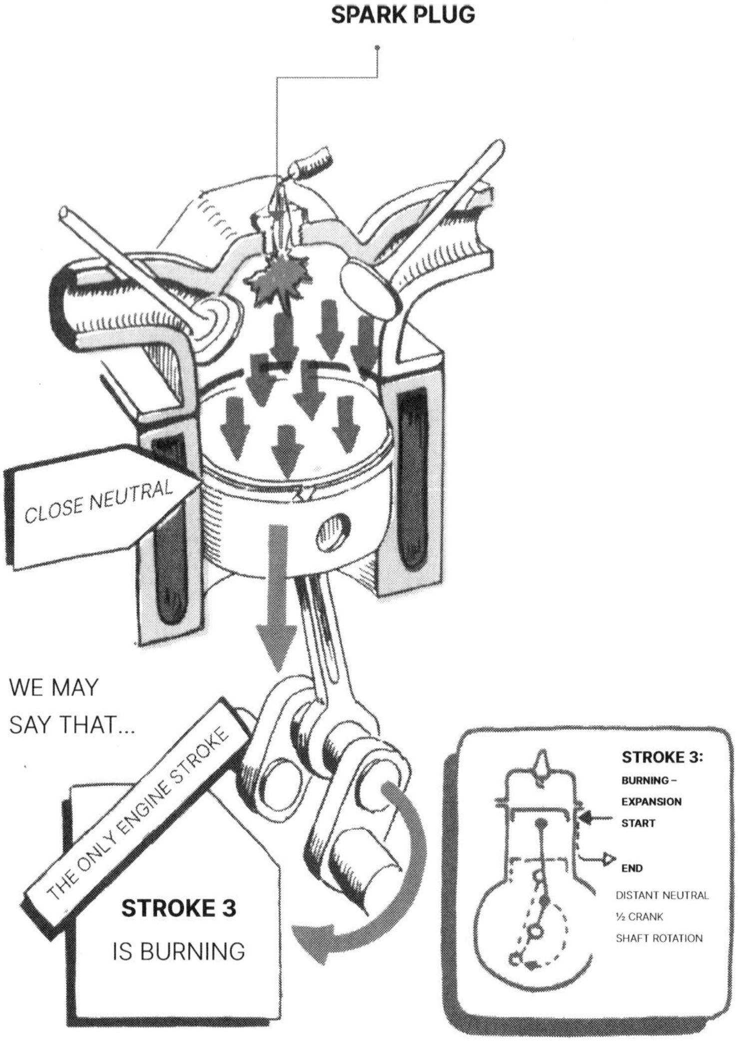

CLOSE NEUTRAL

WE MAY
SAY THAT...

THE ONLY ENGINE STROKE

STROKE 3
IS BURNING

STROKE 3:
BURNING –
EXPANSION
START

END
DISTANT NEUTRAL
½ CRANK
SHAFT ROTATION

The 4 strokes make a complete cycle of the internal combustion 4-stroke engine. A single explosion is produced in a cylinder during a cycle

As one stroke (one piston stroke), corresponds to half a rotation of the crankshaft; it results that in a cylinder

EXHAUSTION VALVE   **EXHAUSTION CHAMBER**

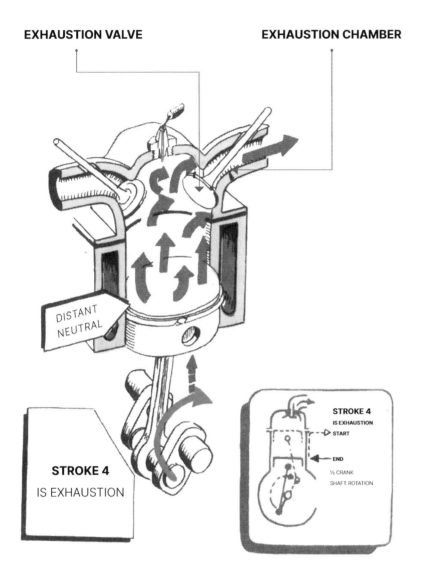

DISTANT
NEUTRAL

STROKE 4

IS EXHAUSTION

STROKE 4
IS EXHAUSTION
➡ START

⬅ END

½ CRANK
SHAFT ROTATION

After expansion of burnt gases, the piston reaches again the close neutral.

The burnt gases being used, have to be exhausted from the cylinder to be replaced by another mixture of gas and air.

To this effect the exhaust valve is opened and the burnt gases exit the cylinder, helped by the piston in its return stroke to the close neutral position.

When exhaustion is ended, the exhaustion valve is closed, and the inlet valve opens and the process repeats.

An explosion is produced at every two rotations of the shaft. During the other 3 strokes the crankshaft is spinned by the explosions of the other cylinders

Of the engine and by the flywheel.

There are also 2-stroke engines, where an explosion is produced in a cylinder at every crankshaft rotation

05

TRANSMISSION SYSTEM

For the 4-stroke engines, the valves open and close at the right moment with the help of a cam shaft spinned by the vilbrochen with the help of two gear wheels named **gearwheels** or through other elements (cogged belts, special chains, etc.)

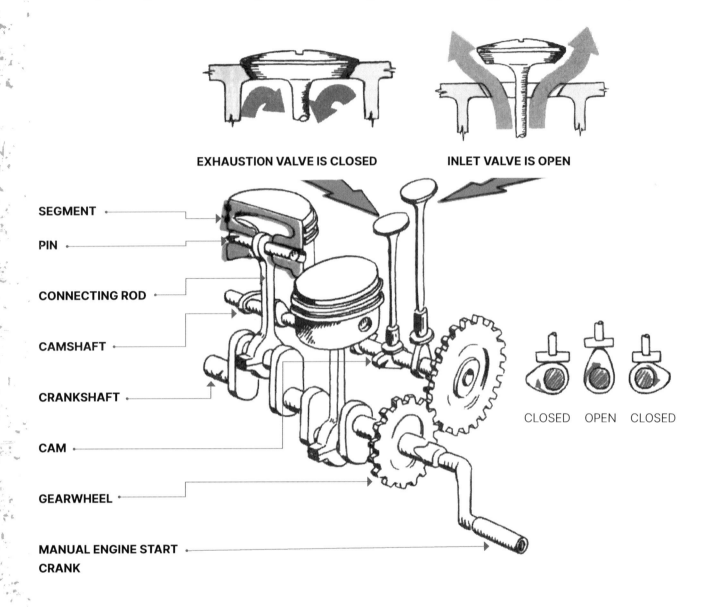

EXHAUSTION VALVE IS CLOSED   **INLET VALVE IS OPEN**

SEGMENT

PIN

CONNECTING ROD

CAMSHAFT

CRANKSHAFT

CAM

GEARWHEEL

MANUAL ENGINE START
CRANK

CLOSED   OPEN   CLOSED

When the cam (oval shaped) is spinning, it lifts the tappet and the valve at the same time, opening the pass for burnt gases and for the fuel-air mixture

Each engine cylinder had 2 valves with 2 cams

All cams are placed on the camshaft

TRANSMISSION SYSTEM

Some engines have cams placed laterally (on the side), others in the cylinder head:

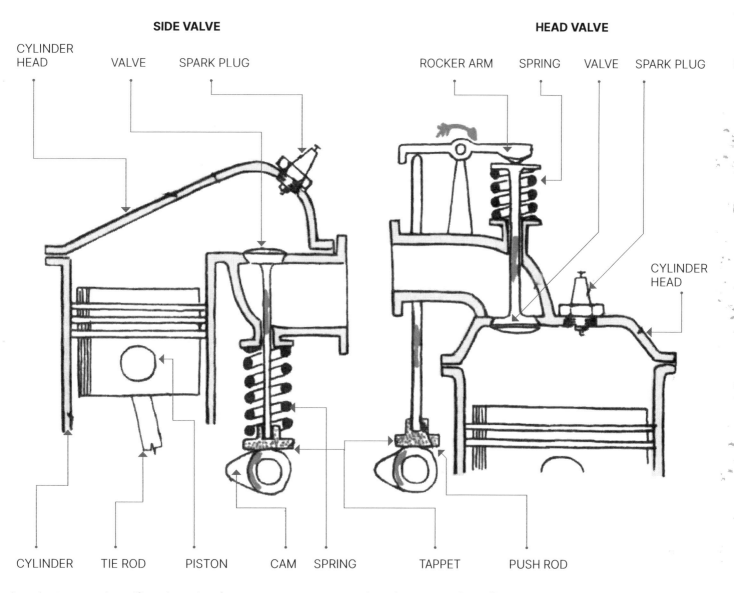

In order to open the orifice, the valve **rises**

The spring helps the immediate closing of the valve, forcing the tappet to stay in permanent contact with the cam on the camshaft this system was used in the construction of old engines (low power)

In order to open the orifice, the valve **lowers** due to the lever arm called **"rocker arm"** which changes the valve motion direction

This system is used for modern engines, that have great power for quite small dimensions

The pinion oh the camshaft must be twice as big as the one on the crankshaft, because for every two crankshaft rotations (at every 4 piston strokes) there is a rotation of the camshaft (a cam is driven)

TWO-STROKE ENGINE

For the two-stroke engine, at every 2 piston strokes (every crankshaft rotation) an explosion is produced moving the engine crankshaft

Inside the engine, different stages take place above and under the piston:

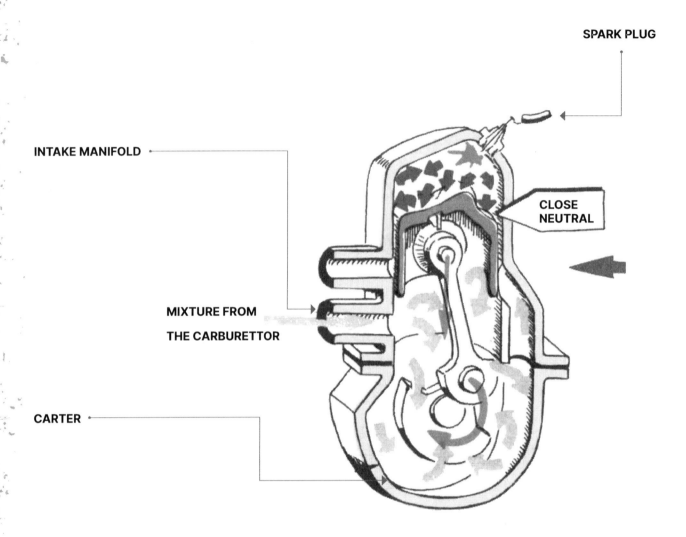

When the piston approaches the close neutral, the spark plug makes an electrical spark, and the mixture compressed in the combustion chamber lights and burns

The intake manifold is emptied **under the piston** as the fuel mixture is sucked into the engine casing (due to the volume increase under the piston, by lifting it)

The pressure of burnt gases pushes the piston, which spins the crankshaft through the tie rod.

EXHAUST MANIFOLD

DEFLECTOR HEAD

SIDE PIPE

The **"sweeping" of the burnt gases** by the fresh ones is called **scavenging**

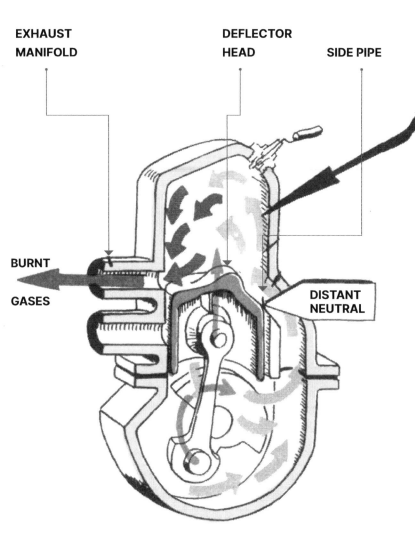

BURNT

GASES

DISTANT NEUTRAL

For some engines the special shape of the piston - (which has a deflector head) – to others the position of the side pipe towards the bottom of the cylinder, favors the scavenging

Compared to the four-stroke engine, the two-stroke engine has the following

WEAKNESSES:

⅄ Greater gasoline consumption;

⅄ The mixing of oil and gasoline, due to the necessity of lubrication leads to great disposals of burning waste on the inside;

⅄ The spark-plug fouling (reduction of electric ignition capacity by shortcircuiting the spark plug insulator due to a deposit of calamine, a conductor deposit) is more frequent because the oil waste adds to gasoline waste ;

⅄ Lower engine performance.

STRENGTHS:

⅄ Simpler and cheaper design, due to the lack of special transmission (valves, camshaft, etc.) And lubrication elements;

⅄ A greater power than a corresponding four-stroke engine

⅄ Easy cold start and impossible to choke (intake made through the carter);

⅄ Easy repairs

During the descent stroke the piston closes the intake manifold and the mixture under the piston (in the casing) is compressed

When approaching the distant neutral, the piston releases the exhaust manifold and then the side pipe through which the cylinder communicates with the casing.

The burnt gases leave the cylinder and the pre-compressed mixture pushes towards the exhaust manifold the rest of the burnt gases from the cylinder

COOLING

A high temperature is generated by burning the gasoline and it is transmitted to the elements near the combustion chamber

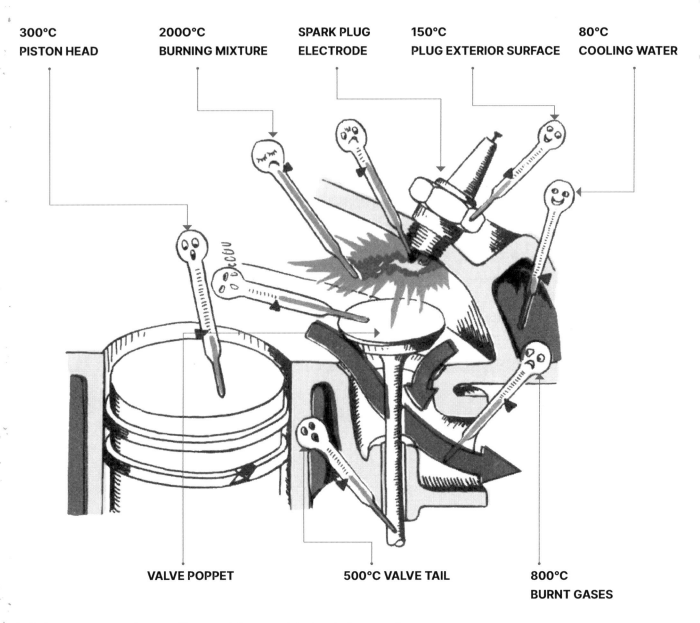

| 300°C | 2000°C | SPARK PLUG | 150°C | 80°C |
| PISTON HEAD | BURNING MIXTURE | ELECTRODE | PLUG EXTERIOR SURFACE | COOLING WATER |

VALVE POPPET   500°C VALVE TAIL   800°C
BURNT GASES

At high temperatures the metallic materials expand, losing their strength

To avoid the overexpansion of the piston and its blockage into the cylinder to increase the duration of engine optimum operation, **it is necessary to cool the engine down**

Cooling the engine **is done** in two ways:

- Directly (or with air)
- Indirectly (or with water)

AIR COOLING

With this system, a part of the heat produced the engine is transmitted directly into the environmental air the air-cooled engine have both the cylinder and the casing equipped on the outside with cooling flanges

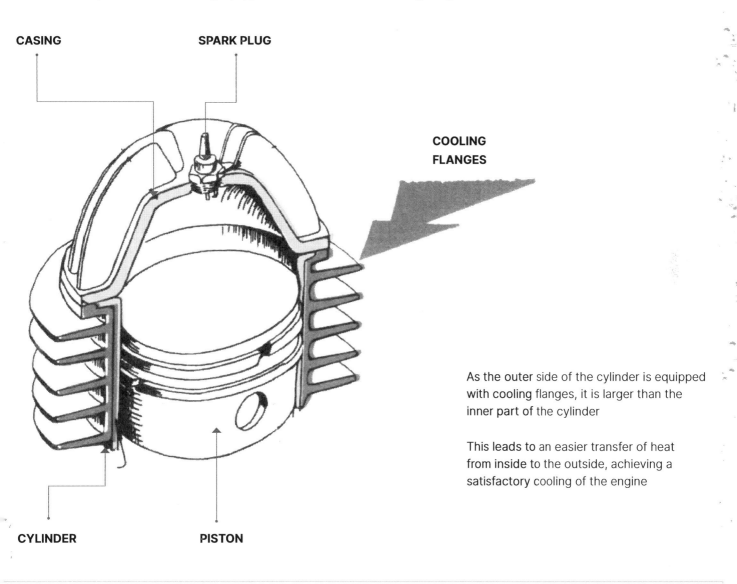

CASING

SPARK PLUG

COOLING FLANGES

CYLINDER

PISTON

As the outer side of the cylinder is equipped with cooling flanges, it is larger than the inner part of the cylinder

This leads to an easier transfer of heat from inside to the outside, achieving a satisfactory cooling of the engine

The air cooling system is adopted for the construction of motorbike engines and of some cars

It brings the advantage of easy building and simple maintenance, easy cold start and lower engine cost still, cooling the engine depends on the temperature and speed of environmental air

To improve cooling, the air speed is increased by air turbines (tatra, trabant, etc.)

WATER COOLING

It is the most used cooling system for car engines

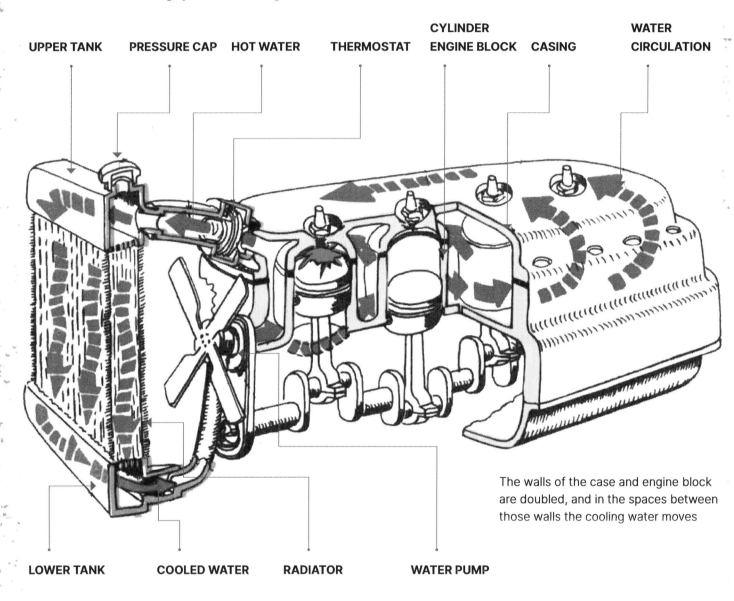

| UPPER TANK | PRESSURE CAP | HOT WATER | THERMOSTAT | CYLINDER ENGINE BLOCK | CASING | WATER CIRCULATION |

The walls of the case and engine block are doubled, and in the spaces between those walls the cooling water moves

| LOWER TANK | COOLED WATER | RADIATOR | WATER PUMP |

As the combustion chambers are on the upper side of the engine, this area heats

THE MOST The water surrounding the combustion chambers shall heat faster and being lighter than the cold water, it will rise towards the radiator, leaving space for the cold water at the cylinder base

The water reaches the radiator, travels through the cooling pipes, enters the engine again in the lower side

A natural circuit of water called **termosiphon** is achieved on this principle

In order to guarantee a good cooling in variour operation situations, the modern engines are equipped with water pumps moved by the crankshaft through a trapezoidal belt

The pump sucks the water in the radiator lower tank and sends it into the engine water chamber, creating a slight overpressure and a forced circulation of water

The thermoregulator is a thermoregulating device that keeps water temperature in the cooling system between 80° and 90°c (the optimum car operating condition experimentally determined)

according to expansion of materials on heat: water cycle when **its temperature is low**, giving water the possibility to remain longer around the combustion chamber , being directed again towards into the pump;

the water **cycle** when its temperature rises above 80°c allowing it to reach the radiator where it can cool

Antifreeze solution is a mixture of alcohol, glycerine and other curing compounds, that has the property to avoid freezing during winter. It is used as a cooling liquid in the cooling system replacing water that freezes during winter, damaging the engine if it is left inside it. Other substance mixtures with similar properties are used. Modern engines are equipped with encapsulated cooling systems that include anti-gel liquid during winter, these engines do no need special care, any freezing danger is excluded, and in summer, liquid boiling is avoided by a manufacturing oversize of the cooling system. The spark plug and the outlet valve cooling are

Modern engines are equipped with encapsulated cooling systems that include anti-gel liquid

During winter, these engines do no need special care, any freezing danger is excluded, and in summer, liquid boiling is avoided by a manufacturing oversize of the cooling system. The spark plug and the outlet valve cooling are

08

LUBRICATION

The engine lubrication achieves the following:

⋏ Reducing friction;
⋏ Cooling bearings;
⋏ Increasing tightness of cylinder segments and walls;
⋏ Driving dust produced by wear;
⋏ Reduction of noise produced by some parts

By turning sprockets the oil is absorbed into the oil pan through the suction

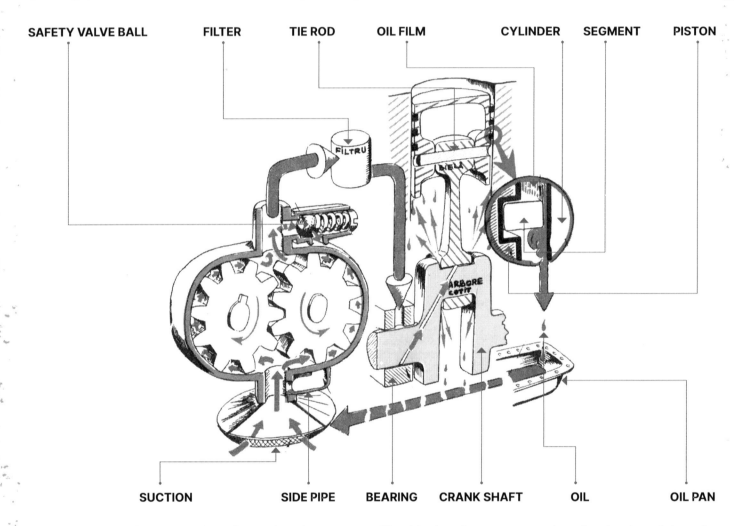

SAFETY VALVE BALL   FILTER   TIE ROD   OIL FILM   CYLINDER   SEGMENT   PISTON

SUCTION   SIDE PIPE   BEARING   CRANK SHAFT   OIL   OIL PAN

The oil in the pump does not go through sprockets, but through the spaces between wheel teeth and the casing wall

Oil, rubbed out by segments on lowering the piston is brought back into the oil pan when it restarts its cycle

Engine lubrication can be performed:

- **By pump**
  For four-stroke engines;
- **By mixture**
  For two-stroke engines;
  Lubrication by mixture consists in mixing oil and gasoline in a 1:33....1:25 Share

BENEFITS:

- Simplified building
- Easy exploitation

DRAWBACKS

- High oil consumption
- Abundant deposits of burning waste and spark plug fouling

LUBRICATION BY PUMP:

The oil pumped by the pump is brought under pressure in the bearing from where it is sent through the orifices of the crankshaft towards the connecting rods, spurts and splashes the surrounding surfaces

The damage of the lubrication system is avoided on increasing engine rotation due to the high oil pressure, through the safety valve : the oil pushes the ball, compresses the spring and then passes through the side pipe back into the lower part of the pump

OIL PROPERTIES

- Viscosity is measured by the draining speed of oil through a certain orifice.
  Unit of measurement : engler degree
- Viscosity index is measured through the variation of viscosity at various temperatures.
  It is measured in deandavis index
- Unctuosity, metal adhesion, oxidation resistance, etc.

Additives are additions of various substances into the oil it improve its qualities. Additivated oils are used in modern engines.

09

ENGINE POWER

Engine power is the most important feature of a vehicle, being influenced by various constructive and functional factors:

CONSTRUCTIVE FACTORS

- Engine capacity
- Compression ratio
- Valves position and shape of combustion chambers
- Spark plug position

FUNCTIONAL FACTORS

- Engine speed
- Tuning quality
- Technical state
- Environmental causes
- Quality of fuel and lubricator

ENGINE CAPACITY

Engine capacity to do the mechanical work (to move the vehicle wheels) is determined by the burning of a quantity of fuel in a certain timespan

The bigger the engine and the greater the quantity of burnt fuel, the greater its power this volume is characterized by the cylinder capacity of engine capacity

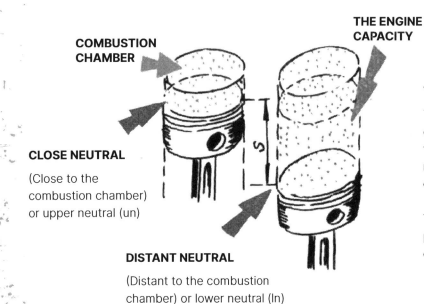

COMBUSTION CHAMBER

THE ENGINE CAPACITY

CLOSE NEUTRAL

(Close to the combustion chamber) or upper neutral (un)

DISTANT NEUTRAL

(Distant to the combustion chamber) or lower neutral (ln)

THE ENGINE CAPACITY

The engine capacity is the volume of the cylinder covered by the active surface of the piston, between the two limit positions in the piston stroke: the close neutral and the distant neutral ...To the combustion chamber

The total cylinder capacity of an engine is given by the product of the capacity of a cylinder and number of cylinders in the engine

COMPRESSION RATIO

Is a constructive feature of the engine, showing how many times the volume occupied by the fuel and air mixture was reduced after compression

$$\text{COMPRESSION RATIO} = \frac{\text{COMBUSTION VOLUME} + \text{CAPACITY}}{\text{COMBUSTION VOLUME}}$$

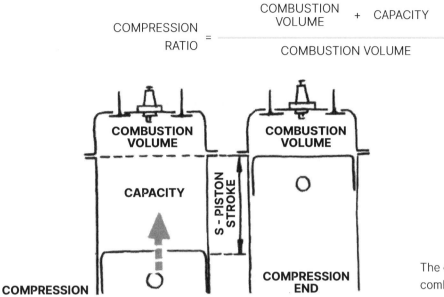

The combustion volume is the combustion chamber volume

The car engines have compression ratios between **4.9 and 9**. The engine power increases proportionally with this ratio, but the compression ratio cannot have exaggerated values due to detonation, a phenomenon happening during the engine operation

---

ENGINE CAPACITY FORMULA

$$V_h = \frac{\pi D^2}{4} \times S \times K$$

Where:

V_h = TOTAL CAPACITY IN L

D = INNER DIAMETER OF A CYLINDER IN dm

S = PISTON STROKE IN dm

K = NUMBER OF ENGINE CYLINDERS

Compression ratio is noted by the greek letter ε (epsilon) and is give by the formula:

$$\Sigma = \frac{V_h + V_A}{V_A} = \frac{V_h}{V_A} + 1$$

Where:

V_h = CYLINDER CAPACITY

V_A = COMBUSTION CHAMBER VOLUME

VALVE LOCATION

The spark plug position and the shape of the combustion chamber also influence the engine power

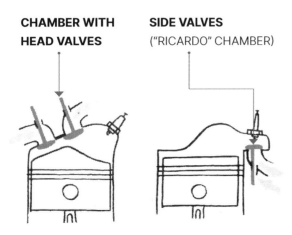

CHAMBER WITH HEAD VALVES

SIDE VALVES ("RICARDO" CHAMBER)

The head valves allow to have a maximum 20% greater power and lower fuel consumption side valves allow to get cheaper engines with transmission elements that produce less noise

FUNCTIONAL FACTORS

They can change the power of the same engine through variation of engine speed and engine tunings, through the variation of environmental conditions (humidity and pressure), road altitude and particularly the qualities of fuel and the vehicle engine power decreases by approx. 10% For each thousand meters altitude and increases during cool seasons

100 HP   90 HP   80 HP

The fuel used for car engines is **gasoline** and it is characterized by

- ┄ Vaporization speed
- ┄ Ignition speed
- ┄ Combustion speed

Detonation is a fast and dangerous burning, as it produces "shock waves" that hit the engine walls and make it vibrate, making this seem like beatings from the outside

Detonation is **promoted** by all causes that increase temperature and pressure during combustion

The octane number is the unit that measures the anti-detonant property of gasoline and is determined by comparing gasoline to a two-substance mixture that have particular detonation trends:

- Isooctane
  Low detonation trend, being attributed the octane number = 100
- Heptane
  High detonation trend, being attributed the octane number = 0

The percentage content of isooctane in the mixture with heptane, at which detonation is produced under the same conditions as those where gasoline is analyzed, **represents the octane number of gasoline**

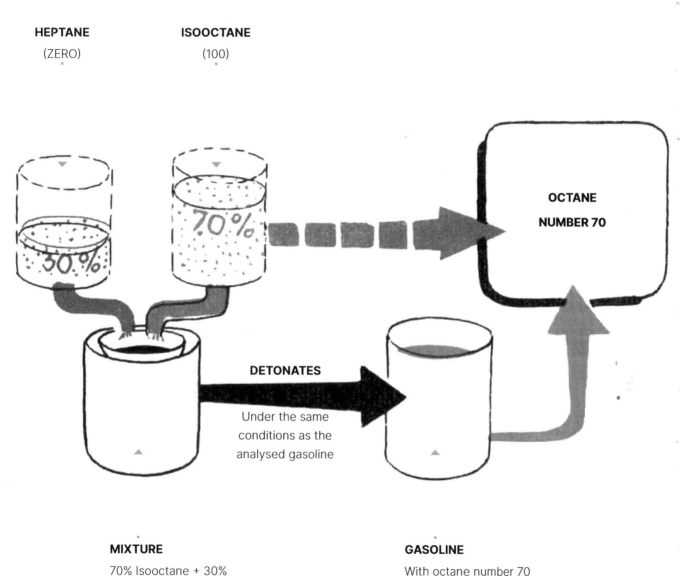

HEPTANE	ISOOCTANE
(ZERO)	(100)

DETONATES

Under the same conditions as the analysed gasoline

OCTANE NUMBER 70

MIXTURE

70% Isooctane + 30%

GASOLINE

With octane number 70

The trial is made with a specially built engine for this purpose

To increase the number, anti-detonant substances (for instance: tetra-ethyl lead = extremely poisonous!) Are mixed with gasoline

The engine power may be calculate by the relation:

THE ENGINE POWER MAY BE CALCULATE BY THE RELATION:

$$P = \frac{V_h \times n \times p}{225 \times i}$$

Where:

P = POWER IN HP

V_h = TOTAL ENGINE CAPACITY IN dm^3

n = ENGINE SPEED IN RPM

p = Mean effective pressure of the cylinder in KCf/cm^3 (at current engines p=7....10 KGf/cm^3)

i = NUMBER OF ENGINE STROKES

It results that **the two-stroke engine**, having as denominator 225 × 2= 450, theoretically it will be **two times more powerful than the four-stroke engine**, with the same characteristics, as the relation numerator shall be in this case twice as big, that is 225 × 4 = 900 the average pressure in the cylinder is determined by the compression Ratio ε

The rated capacity is the maximum power of the engine measured under standardized conditions

The catalogs made according to german standards (din) measure the power of the completely equipped engine with fan, air cleaner, muffler, water pump and dynamo (which absorb part of the engine power) while the american and english norms (s.A.E.) Stipulate the measurement of engine power without the mentioned accessories.

COOLING SYSTEM   WATER PUMP   AIR FILTER

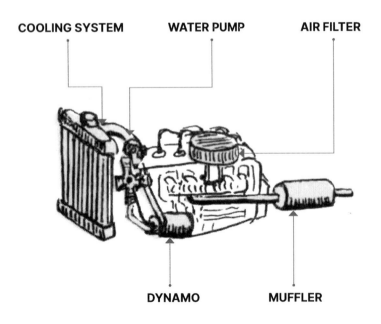

DYNAMO   MUFFLER

It results that the power of the same engine, measured according to s.A.E. Shall be around 10...20% greater than the one measured according to din or stas

The engine power may be determined at **the test bench**, using

$$P = \frac{M \times n}{7162}$$

Where:

P = POWER IN HP

M = TORQUE IN KGfm; MEASURED AT THE TEST BENCH

n = ENGINE SPEED IN RPM

The test bench is made of a stand where the trial engine is placed, a coupling system and a mechanical, hydraulic or electric brake, that makes it possible for the torque to be measured (in kilogram-force-meter)

The torque represents an important feature of an engine

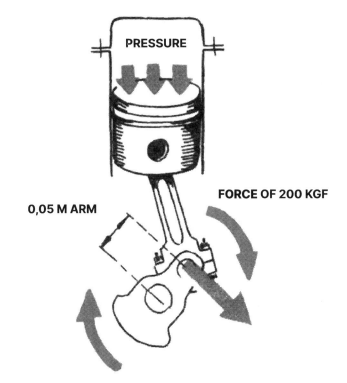

PRESSURE

0,05 M ARM

FORCE OF 200 KGF

TORQUE OF 200 X 0.05= 10 KGFM

It appears due to the pressure of burnt gases, exercised on the piston and transmitted through the tie rod, to the engine crankshaft

The torques is influenced by the force pushing on the piston and by the crankshaft crankpin arm. The size of the torque

Determines the capacity of the vehicle to **climb ramps** without using lower combinations (gears) of the gearbox

The value of the maximum torque is between 7 kgfm (small cars) and up to 22 kgfm (big limos) reaching 45kgfm for heavy trucks

For all engines the speed at maximum torque is lower than the torque at maximum power

10

THE CLUTCH

It is the first transmission element of the vehicle and it functions based on the principle of rotational motion transmission by the friction of contacting surfaces:

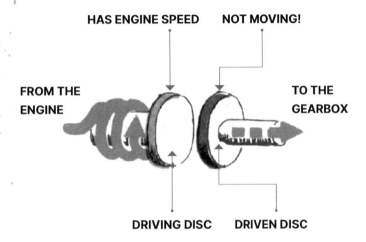

HAS ENGINE SPEED NOT MOVING!

FROM THE ENGINE TO THE GEARBOX

DRIVING DISC DRIVEN DISC

As long as the clutch **discs** are **distant**, the engine rotational motion is not transmitted the engine works, but the connection with the other transmission elements is interrupted and the vehicle does not move

At the beginning of torque, when discs are close, they rub against each other, the driving disc spins at great speed, and the driven disc starts spinning at low speed, that is it slips

If the gearbox is coupled, thevehicle starts smoothly

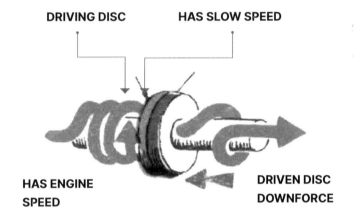

DRIVING DISC HAS SLOW SPEED

HAS ENGINE SPEED DRIVEN DISC DOWNFORCE

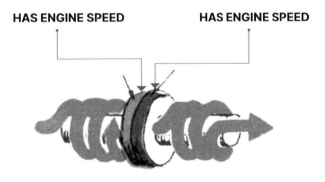

HAS ENGINE SPEED HAS ENGINE SPEED

When the two discs reach **the same speed**, the driven disc stops slipping the vehicle moves at greater speed

HAS ENGINE SPEED IT STOPS

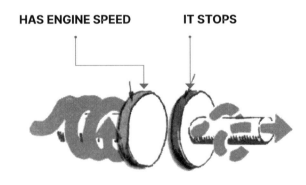

- ⌁ On clutch **decoupling**, the discs drift apart (under the influence of pedal pushing force)
- ⌁ The vehicle can be stopped sharply, while the engine keeps working
- ⌁ The clutch protects the engine elements from the consequences

The role of the clutch is:

- ↟ To couple progressively the engine with the other car elements on starting the car, allowing a smooth start;
- ↟ To decouple sharply the engine from the transmission elements of the car, on stopping the car, giving the engine the possibility to keep working;
- ↟ To allow the change of the gears in the gearbox without shocks, by decoupling transmission.

The material used for the construction of the friction discs of common clutches must have certain qualities imposed by the working conditions:

- ↟ To have a high friction coefficient, that will allow the transmission of the rotational motion;
- ↟ To keep its qualities even at high temperatures, produced by the friction happening during the clutch operation

A special material is used – plane asbestos and metal gaskets - named **metal-asbestos**

The clutch disc, also named driven disc for construction and exploitation reasons has the following parts:

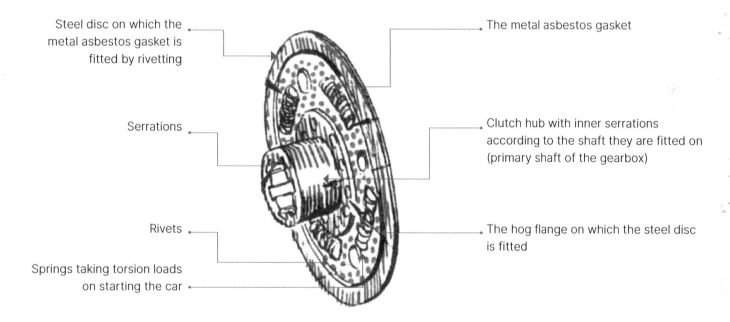

Steel disc on which the metal asbestos gasket is fitted by rivetting

The metal asbestos gasket

Serrations

Clutch hub with inner serrations according to the shaft they are fitted on (primary shaft of the gearbox)

Rivets

The hog flange on which the steel disc is fitted

Springs taking torsion loads on starting the car

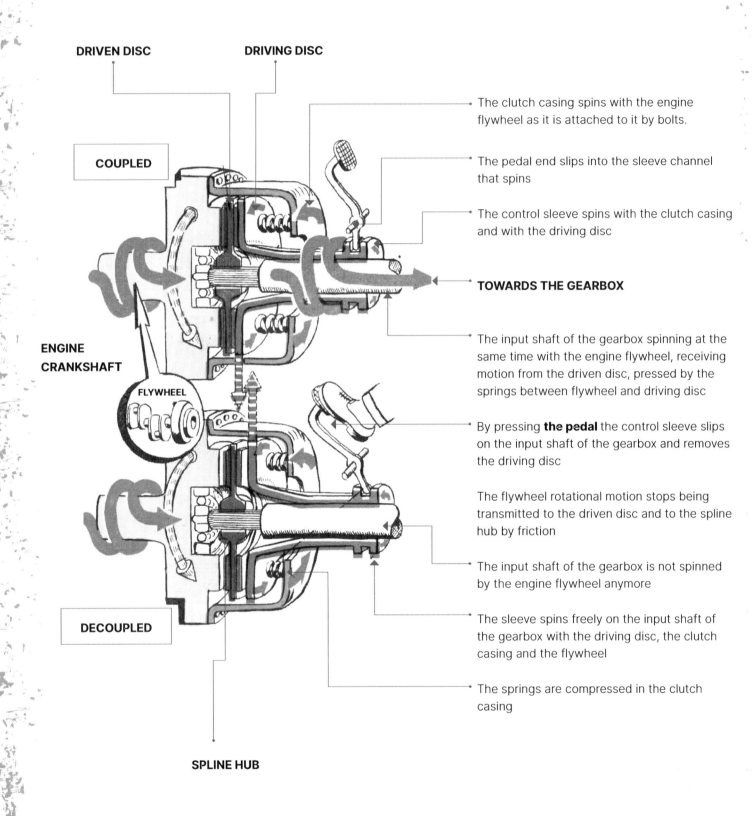

DRIVEN DISC

DRIVING DISC

COUPLED

ENGINE
CRANKSHAFT

FLYWHEEL

DECOUPLED

SPLINE HUB

The clutch casing spins with the engine flywheel as it is attached to it by bolts.

The pedal end slips into the sleeve channel that spins

The control sleeve spins with the clutch casing and with the driving disc

TOWARDS THE GEARBOX

The input shaft of the gearbox spinning at the same time with the engine flywheel, receiving motion from the driven disc, pressed by the springs between flywheel and driving disc

By pressing **the pedal** the control sleeve slips on the input shaft of the gearbox and removes the driving disc

The flywheel rotational motion stops being transmitted to the driven disc and to the spline hub by friction

The input shaft of the gearbox is not spinned by the engine flywheel anymore

The sleeve spins freely on the input shaft of the gearbox with the driving disc, the clutch casing and the flywheel

The springs are compressed in the clutch casing

The friction of the pedal end and the sleeve is eliminated through lever systems and a pressure bearing

Most clutches have a dry friction of contact discs. Motorbikes use clutches that have oil-drowned discs

The pedal effort is reduced by a system of levers which allows a better placement of the driver's seat

In some modern vehicles the clutch feed control is hydraulic or electromechanical

Other modern constructions have **hydraulic clutches** with slow couplings, functioning by the circulation of oil between the vanes of a pump and a hydraulic turbine

The clutch **hydraulic control** is used for modern vehicles, being meant to reduce effort on pedal. It is operated in the same way as the hydraulic brake : on pressing the pedal, the pressure created within the main pump is transmitted to the receptor cylinder, where the piston rod **decouples** the clutch

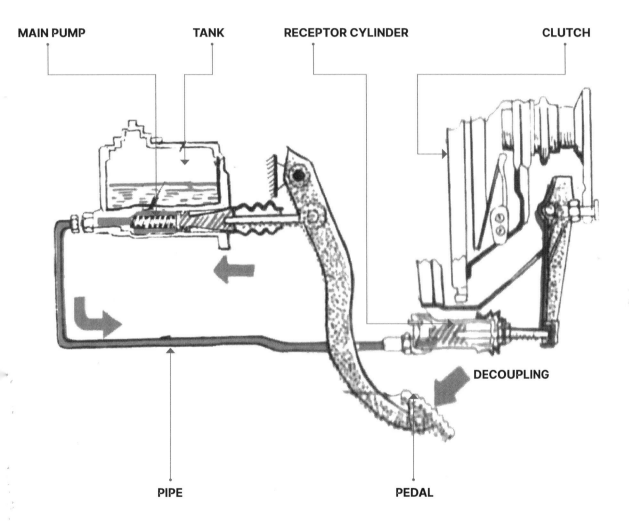

THE GEARBOX

Is the element which allows the vehicle to:

⮝ Start moving at low speed and high engine speed;
⮝ Reverse direction (backwards) without being necessary to change the crankshaft spinning course
⮝ Park while the engine is running and without pressing the clutch pedal.

It functions based on the principle of transmission of rotational motion through the gear wheels, also named sprockets, a driving one and a driven one

These **gears** may keep or change the engine speed:

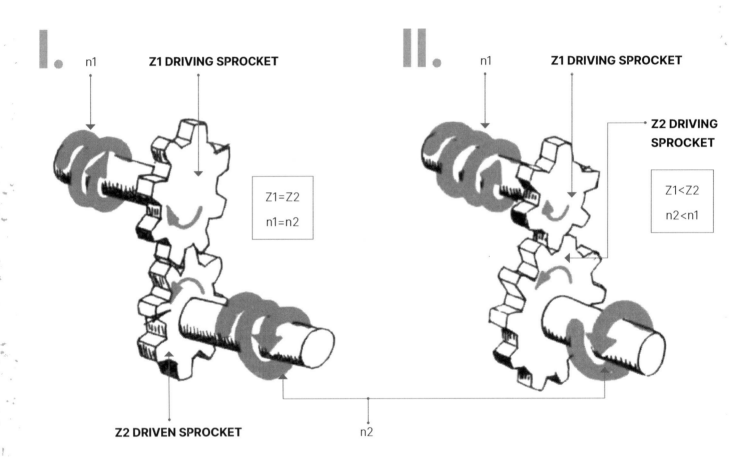

I.

n1   **Z1 DRIVING SPROCKET**

$$Z1 = Z2$$
$$n1 = n2$$

Z2 DRIVEN SPROCKET   n2

II.

n1   **Z1 DRIVING SPROCKET**

Z2 DRIVING SPROCKET

$$Z1 < Z2$$
$$n2 < n1$$

When the 2 sprockets have the same size (the same number of teeth z1= z2) the gear speed does not change (n1=n2)

The transmission formula is said to be

$$i = \frac{n1}{n2} = \frac{Z2}{Z1} = 1$$

The rotation is reversed

When the driving sprocket is smaller (it has less teeth z1<z2) the gear is **reducing** (decrease)

The driven sprocket speed is lower (n2<n1) and reverse

The transmission formula is higher than 1:

$$i = \frac{n1}{n2} = \frac{Z2}{Z1} > 1$$

When the driving sprocket is bigger, it has more teeth (z1>z2) the gear is **multiplying**

The driven sprocket speed is higher (n2>n1) and reverse

The transmission formula is lower than 1:

$$i = \frac{n1}{n2} = \frac{Z2}{Z1} < 1$$

When an **intermediate sprocket** (z2) is introduced between the driving one (z1) and the driven one (z3), the **rotation direction** of the driven sprocket **is the same** with that of the driving sprocket (z1)

The transmission formula depends of z2 and z3:

$$i = \frac{Z3}{Z1}$$

III.

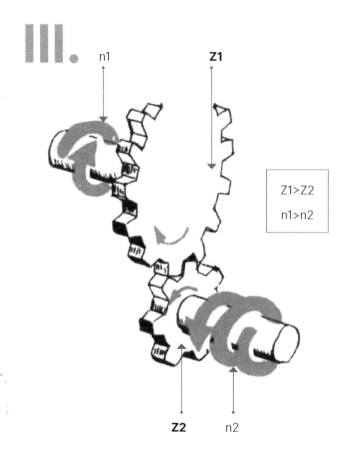

n1   **Z1**

Z1>Z2
n1>n2

Z2   n2

IV.

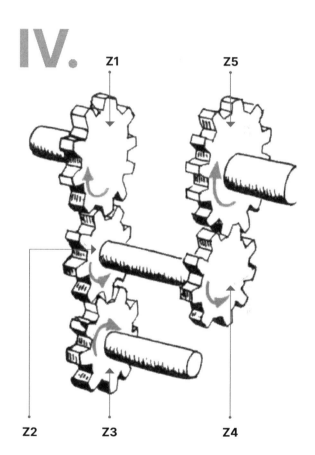

Z1   **Z5**

Z2   **Z3**   **Z4**

The gearboxes have linkages that transmit the rotational motion by coupling several sprockets, for instance: z1-z2-z4-z5, some of them being rooted on the same shaft and having the same speed (Z4 and Z2 in figure iv)

In order to **reverse the rotational direction** of vehicle drive wheels (going backwards), an extra sprocket is placed in the linkage

The coupling of various sprocket combinations achieves various speeds of the vehicle, ordered through a system of levers, by the gear lever

THE OPERATION

The operation of a gearbox with:

The gear lever may be placed within the floor (in classical vehicles and full back vehicles) or on the wheel (in classical vehicles and full front vehicles)

The synchronizer is a mechanism that is meant to balance the driven shaft speed with that of the input shaft before coupling the sprockets, so that it can operate without teeth snatching, hence without noise

Some vehicles have gearboxes with 4 gears for forward movement and one gear for reverse movement

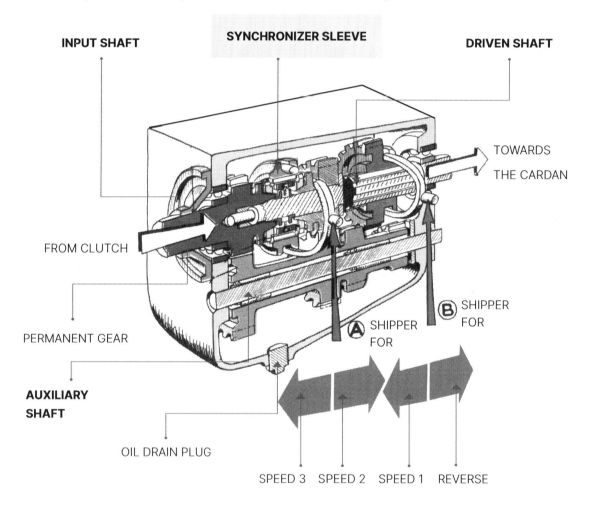

INPUT SHAFT

SYNCHRONIZER SLEEVE

DRIVEN SHAFT

TOWARDS THE CARDAN

FROM CLUTCH

PERMANENT GEAR

(A) SHIPPER FOR

(B) SHIPPER FOR

AUXILIARY SHAFT

OIL DRAIN PLUG

SPEED 3   SPEED 2   SPEED 1   REVERSE

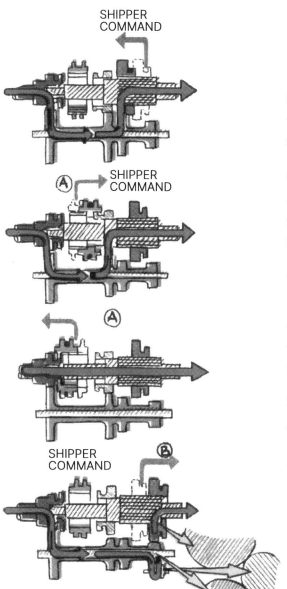

GEAR 1

The b shipper couples the sprocket on the driven shaft with its pair on the auxiliary shaft

GEAR 2

The a shipper couples the synchronizer sleeve through its lower teeth to the outer teeth of the driven shaft sprocket, permanently coupled to its pair on the auxiliary shaft

GEAR 3

(DIRECT GEAR)

The a shipper couples the synchronizer sleeve through its inner teeth to the outer teeth of the driving shaft sprocket, permanently coupled to its pair on the auxiliary shaft

REVERSE

The b shipper couples the sprocket on the driven shaft with its pair on the reverse gear shaft, which is permanently coupled to the last sprocket on the auxiliary shaft

THE CARDANIC TRANSMISSION

It transmits the rotational motion from the gearbox to the drive wheels

To the classical vehicles that have the engine located at the front and the drive wheels at the back **the cardanic transmission crosses the entire vehicle,** from the gearbox to the differential

IT IS MADE OF

Cardan crosses are necessary to allow the transmission of rotational motion under various angles made by the propeller shaft, due to the suspension oscillation cycles while the car is moving

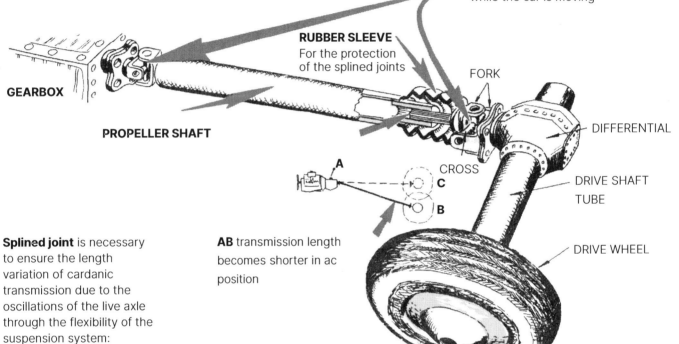

GEARBOX

RUBBER SLEEVE
For the protection of the splined joints

FORK

PROPELLER SHAFT

DIFFERENTIAL

A

CROSS

C

B

DRIVE SHAFT TUBE

DRIVE WHEEL

Splined joint is necessary to ensure the length variation of cardanic transmission due to the oscillations of the live axle through the flexibility of the suspension system:

AB transmission length becomes shorter in ac position

TUNNEL

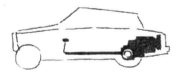

CLASSICAL SOLUTION:

Requires the Existence of cardanic Transmission, which is a Disadvantage for the use of the Interior space

MODERN SOLUTIONS

Full back and especially full front eliminate the tunnel crossing the vehicle, offering advantages by reducing the cost of the vehicle and increasing the interior space, lowering at the same time the center of gravity

THE DIFFERENTIAL

Is a mechanism which transmits the rotational motion to the drive wheels, allowing them to spin at various speeds in turns

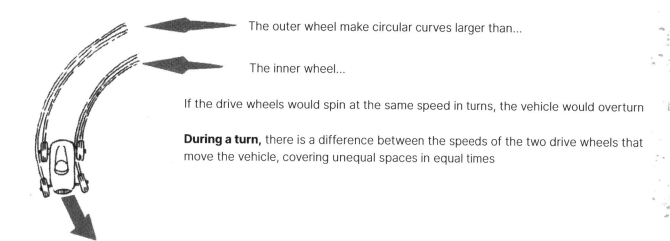

The outer wheel make circular curves larger than...

The inner wheel...

If the drive wheels would spin at the same speed in turns, the vehicle would overturn

During a turn, there is a difference between the speeds of the two drive wheels that move the vehicle, covering unequal spaces in equal times

THE DIFFERENTIAL IS MADE OF :

The crown gear spinning freely on the drive shafts with the differential pinion casing

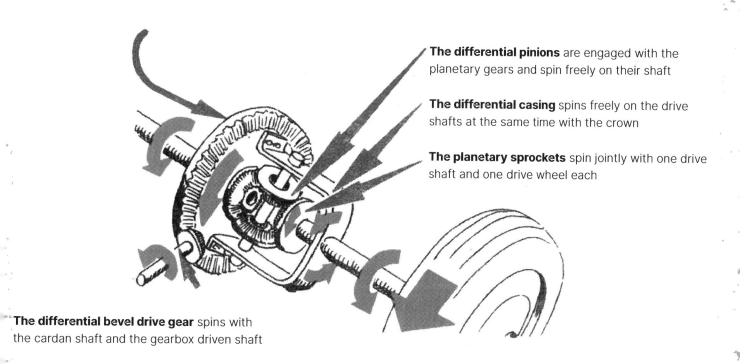

The differential pinions are engaged with the planetary gears and spin freely on their shaft

The differential casing spins freely on the drive shafts at the same time with the crown

The planetary sprockets spin jointly with one drive shaft and one drive wheel each

The differential bevel drive gear spins with the cardan shaft and the gearbox driven shaft

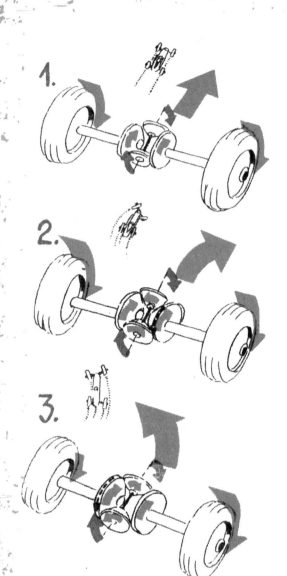

I.

ON FLAT GROUND

The right planetary sprockets (PD) and the left ones (PS) spin at an equal speed with the rolling of the differential pinions shaft the differential pinions do not spin, but roll with their shaft (following the direction of the blue arrows)

II.

TURNING RIGHT

The speed of the right planetary sprocket (NPD) is lower than the speed of the one on the left (NPS)

$$NPD < NPS$$

The differential pinions roll and spin around their axis, increasing the speed of the left planetary sprocket with the slip of the right one

III.

TURNING LEFT

The speed of the left planetary sprocket (NPS) is lower than the speed of the one on the left (NPD)

$$NPS < NPD$$

The differential pinions Roll and spin around Their axis, increasing the Speed of the right Planetary sprocket with The slip of the left one

11

SUSPENSION SYSTEM

The suspension has the function of transforming shocks caused by road irregularities in oscillations of the vehicle, easy to stand by the passengers an imaginary pencil placed on the body of a vehicle would draw on a side wall its vertical oscillations:

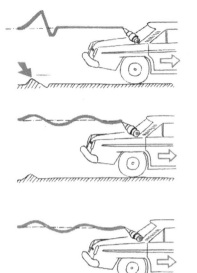

NO SUSPENSION

The shock would be transmitted to the entire body of the vehicle as a jolt obstacle

SUSPENSION

Turns the shock into sustained oscillations of the body

THE DAMPER

Reduces sustained oscillations into short and easy to take oscllationsturns the shock into sustained oscillations of the body

SUSPENSION IS ACHIEVED THROUGH :

- Elastic elements of the suspension system;
- Tyres and their inner tubes;
- Suspension system dampers;
- The upholstered chairs of the vehicle

THE ELASTIC ELEMENTS OF THE SUSPENSION CAN INCLUDE:

- Leaf springs;
- Coil springs;
- Torsion rods;
- Rubber buffers and pneumatic cylinders (less used)

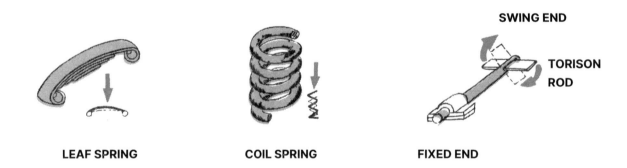

LEAF SPRING   **COIL SPRING**   **SWING END** **TORISON ROD** **FIXED END**

The suspension may be built either with a rigid axle or with independent wheels

WITH RIGID AXLE

Used in old vehicles, where leaf springs are predominant

The oscillations of one wheel influence the position of the entire vehicle

WITH INDEPENDENT WHEELS

Used in modern vehicles, with coil or leaf springs

The oscillations of one wheel do not change the position of the other wheel

THE INDEPENDENT SUSPENSION

Is adopted by all modern vehicles, being made in different building variants:

WITH OSCILLATING DRIVE SHAFTS:

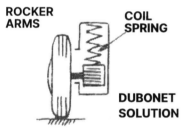

PATH

CROSS LEAF SPRINGS

ROCKER ARMS   **COIL SPRING**

DUBONET SOLUTION

They are made with leaf springs, coil springs or torsion rods. When wheels oscillate, their route and tilt vary, producing an increased wear of the tyres

With two cross

With one cross leaf spring (upper or lower) and rocker arms leaf springs

These solutions are adopted to low power vehicles

Independent Telescopic Suspension

Parallelogram Style Suspension

On oscillation of wheels, the route and toe in vary, but the caster and camber stay constant

Has an inner coil spring and it is beneficial, as during wheel oscillations, the specific angles stay constant

Includes coil springs, torsion rods or buffers and are used in most of modern vehicles

It is made of the following main parts:

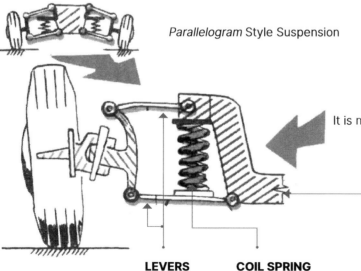

BODY-FRAME

LEVERS   **COIL SPRING**

CAR DAMPER

Car damper The modern one is telescopic and has a double action:

- It offers low resistance when the wheel gets close to the frame
- It offers high resistance when the wheel moves away from the frame

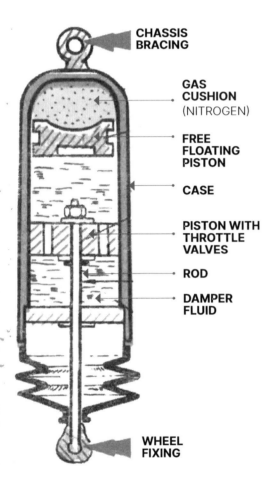

CHASSIS BRACING

GAS CUSHION (NITROGEN)

FREE FLOATING PISTON

CASE

PISTON WITH THROTTLE VALVES

ROD

DAMPER FLUID

WHEEL FIXING

THE BENEFITS OF THE TELESCOPIC DAMPER

Compared to other dampers (with levers):

- Reduced volume, simple and cheap building;
- May be installed inside the coil spring;
- Is it light and makes no noise

The gas-cushion shock absorber is used for the latest vehicles, offering functional **advantages**, such as: optimum comfort, eliminating hits in maximum strokes, etc)

When the wheel **gets close** to the frame, the rod lifts and forces the liquid to go through the throttle valves. The free-floating piston is pulled upwards, compressing the gas

When the wheel **moves away** from the frame, the rod lowers and forces the liquid to return above the piston with throttle valves stopping the oscillations. Under the pressure of nitrogen, the free-floating piston comes back to the initial position

The buffer piston and **the gas cushion** eliminate the hits on long strokes

The "mc pherson" suspension combines the telescopic suspension with an incorporated hydraulic damper, being used to some modern vehicles (ford, bmw, porsche, etc.)

It is a special oil with low viscosity, low freezing point, having anti-foaming, anti-oxidation addtives, etc. It may be replaced with an equal parts mixture of insulating oil and turbine oil.

12

THE STEERING SYSTEM

The steering mechanism allows the vehicle to turn

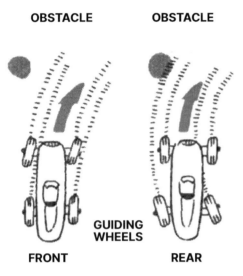

OBSTACLE   OBSTACLE

GUIDING WHEELS

FRONT   REAR

The common cars have **the steering system placed on its two front wheels**, as the driver may see during turning, the outer points of the car body. The rear wheels leave traces on the inside of the turn

The steering placed on the rear wheels is rarely adopted by some special utility vehicles (with rear wheels leaving traces on the outside of the turn)

The requirements of the steering system are the following:

⊥ Allow the appropriate wheel rolling, without influence from the suspension oscillation
⊥ Easy and safe actuation without extra effort of the driver
⊥ After the turn and the attenuation of the effort on the wheel , the wheels come back to straight position
⊥ Not to become easily disturbed

The specific angles of the wheels are manufactured in order to guarantee a proper operation. One can identify: the caster angle, the camber angle, the toe-in, sai, scrub radius

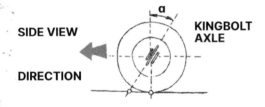

SIDE VIEW

DIRECTION

KINGBOLT AXLE

The caster angle α - between the vertical and the kingbolt axle. Its role is to straighten the steering wheels after the turn and the loosened effort on the wheel

Maximum tilt of the kingbolt axle 9°30'

The need for caster is determined by the tendency of a wheel to position itself so that road contact point b would be placed behind point a (the intersection of the pivot axle extension and the road)

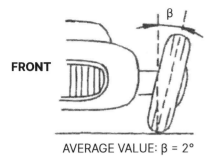

FRONT

AVERAGE VALUE: β = 2°

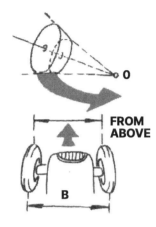

FROM ABOVE

B

The wheel closing is measured in mm: C=B-A

The camber β between a longitudinal vertical section and the wheel symmetry plane. It increases stability, prevents pendular movement, strenghtens the wheel stress on the big bearing, decreasing the wear of the drive wheels bearings.

But the deformation of tyres and the camber determine a **toe-out** rolling of the wheel, similar to that of a cone , which needs to be reduced

The toe-in C is the front closing angle of the driving wheels and has the role of reducing the divergent rolling tendency, due to the camber and to the pivot being pushed at the rear-wheel drive vehicles. It is wrongly named caster.

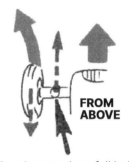

FROM ABOVE

The pivot tends to fall behind

At the front-wheel drive vehicles, the pivot tends to fall behind, generating a toe-in rolling.

In these vehicles the toe-in is negative (the wheels are "open" to maximum values of the toe-in:

- ⊥ + 6 mm (rear-wheel drive)
- ⊥ - 6 mm (front-wheel drive)

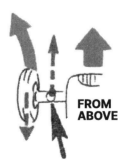

FROM ABOVE

The pivot tends to fall behind

THE STEERING AXIS INCLINATION

READ DELTA **FROM THE FRONT**

DIRECTION

CONTACT SPOT

LONGITUDINAL AXIS

KINGBOLT AXLE

PIVOT AXLE

Brings the extension of the swivel close to the wheel contact with the road

Turning, increases security during driving and reduces wear in the steering system maximum values : 9°30'

The scrub radius is measured in mm on the contact spot of the tyre with the road

The exension of the pivot pin meets the road on the contact spot at a d distance from the longitudinal axis of the spot, the distance is called scrub radius.

Maximum value : 30 mm

Some modern vehicles have reduces almost totally the caster, the camber and the toe-in, keeping the sai and the scrub radius.

The steering system of a **rigid axle** vehicle is made of:

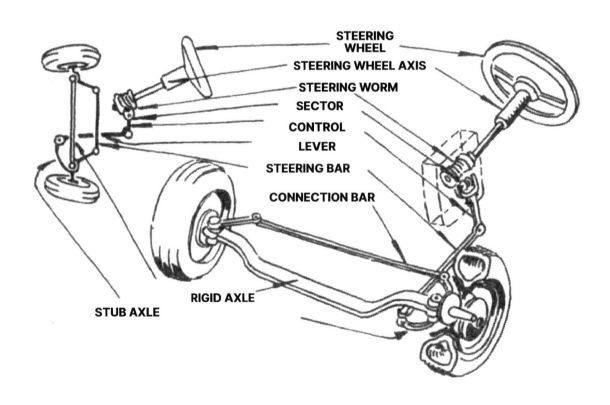

STEERING WHEEL

STEERING WHEEL AXIS

STEERING WORM

SECTOR

CONTROL LEVER

STEERING BAR

CONNECTION BAR

STUB AXLE

RIGID AXLE

The steering system of an **independent suspension** vehicle is made of fewer elements:

In modern vehicles the control lever directly actuates the connection bar, eliminating the steering bar

Thus space is saved and manufacture is simplified

To increase safety while driving and to avoid changes to driving wheel specific angles, the connection bar is made of several bent segments

The steering gear box includes the reducing gear of the wheel rotational movement

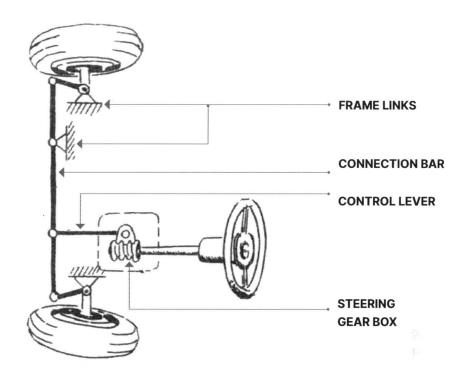

FRAME LINKS

CONNECTION BAR

CONTROL LEVER

STEERING
GEAR BOX

To most vehicles this mechanism is made of worm and roller (the roller allows the rolling of a sector instead of friction, so that the rapid wear of the mechanism can be avoided)

There are also steering mechanisms with rack and pinion, with ball nut, etc.

Some vehicles have hydraulic servomechanisms that make driving much easier.

Steering wheel on the left side has benefits for right - hand traffic (visibility in overtaking, at crossroads, etc)

13

BRAKES

The role of the braking system is to:

- Slow the car speed or stop the vehicle
- To secure the vehicle parking on flat ground or on slope

Any vehicle is equipped with **two independent** braking **mechanisms**:

- Handbrake or central brake (for arking), which blocks the cardan shaft or the rear wheels, through levers
- Foot brake or service brake that actuate on all wheels of the vehicle through a mechanical, hydraulic or pneumatic process

Almost all modern vehicles are equipped with **hydraulic** foot brakes.

Braking the rotational movement is achieved by:

- A band (in some handbrakes);
- Blocks (in handbrakes and particularly in foot brakes);
- Discs (in foot brakes for some modern vehicles)

BAR BAND	BLOCK	DISC

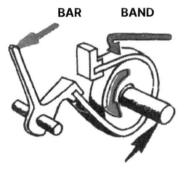

Link to the cardan shaft

BLOCK

Drum spins with the wheel

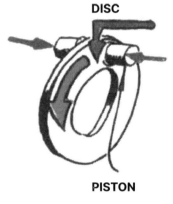

PISTON

By controlling the bar, the band tightens around a disc or drum stopping it from rotation

By pressing the block, it rubs the interior of the drum stopping it from rotation

The disc is stopped by pressing the pistons on it

The material that comes into contact and rubs the moving part, must meet certain conditions:

- Have a high coefficient of friction (not to facilitate sliding);
- Not to produce noise and not to wear fast;
- Behave well in high temperature variations, etc.

Metal asbestos is used. It is made of asbestos with wire insertions. It is also used in clutches, but in other forms, as plane fittings

The minimum braking distance of the vehicle depends on several factors, such as:

- The vehicle speed;
- The road state, the brake quality;
- The driver's skill, etc.

This distance may be approximately determined using the chart below (also named nomogram), with perfectly operational brakes and a well-skilled driver.

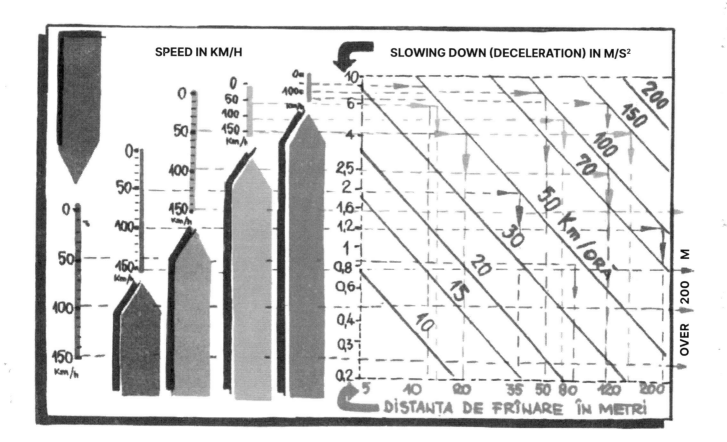

OPERATION OF THE HYDRAULIC BRAKE

It is based on pascal's principle

On pressing the pedal, its back-moving spring is pushed and the bar pushes the piston into the central cylinder pump, where liquid is compressed

The liquid pressure is transmitted through pipes to wheel slave cylinders, where they act on pistons that they make move away. The piston rods push in their turn the blocks towards the wheel drums, that they stop from their rotational motion, stopping the vehicle.

On lifting the foot from the pedal, its back-moving spring brings the pedal back to its initial position and with it, the piston of the central pump.

The lack of pressure in the slave cylinder makes the blocks backmoving spring to bring the blocks into the initial position, making it move away from the wheel drum and slowing the stopping.

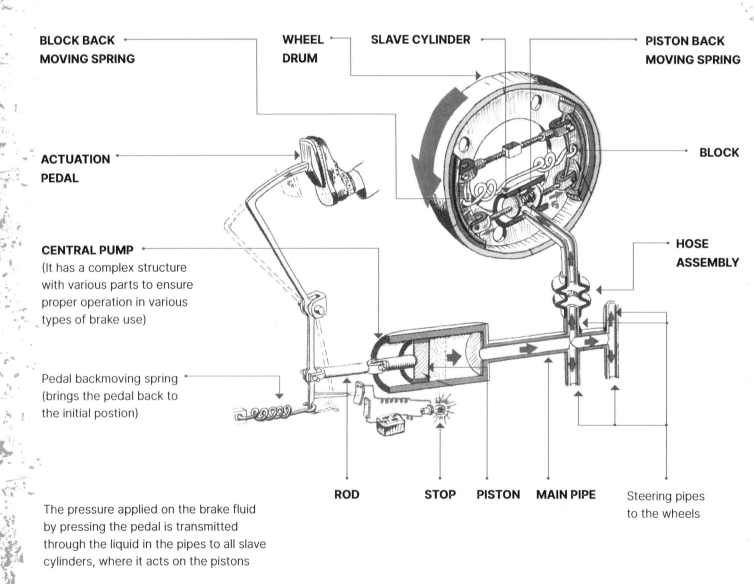

BLOCK BACK MOVING SPRING

WHEEL DRUM

SLAVE CYLINDER

PISTON BACK MOVING SPRING

ACTUATION PEDAL

BLOCK

CENTRAL PUMP
(It has a complex structure with various parts to ensure proper operation in various types of brake use)

HOSE ASSEMBLY

Pedal backmoving spring
(brings the pedal back to the initial postion)

ROD　　**STOP**　　**PISTON**　　**MAIN PIPE**　　Steering pipes to the wheels

The pressure applied on the brake fluid by pressing the pedal is transmitted through the liquid in the pipes to all slave cylinders, where it acts on the pistons

There are numerous advantages of using hydraulic brakes:

- They are noiseless
- They stop all wheels progressively and equally
- No special attention needed

Brake fluid must:

- Vaporize at high temperatures (Over +150°C)
- Freeze at low temperatures (Below -50°C)Have a viscosity as constant as possible on temperature variations
- Not form clots that may block pipes
- Not to enter a chemical reaction with the materials of the parts in contact

The silicone fluid is used as brake fluid, fulfilling the requirements. In the absence of original brake fluid, various mixtures may be used such as castor oil or glycerine and alcohol, with satisfactory results

---

PASCAL'S PRINCIPLE

Any pressure from the outside exercised over a liquid is completely transmitted to any surface in contact with the liquid.

$$p = \frac{F1}{S1} = \frac{F2}{S2}$$

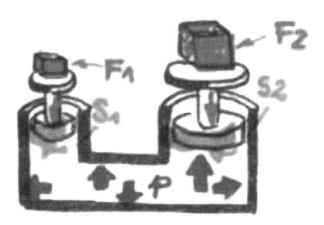

Under the action of the F1 force the pistons will stay in balance if the F2 force opposes the F1

14

THE DISC BRAKE

It is used in modern vehicles having the following **main benefits:**

- Allows the reduction of wheel weight
- Work well in any conditions
- Allows an easy replacement of gaskets
- No noise is produces while using the brakes

In order to evacuate more easily the heat, some modern cars have wheel drums made of aluminum alloys

The disc brake is based on the same hydraulic principle as the block hydraulic brake

On pushing the pedal, the fluid pressure actuates on pistons that push the two gasket plates towards the side surfaces of the drum disc, stopping it from its rotational motion

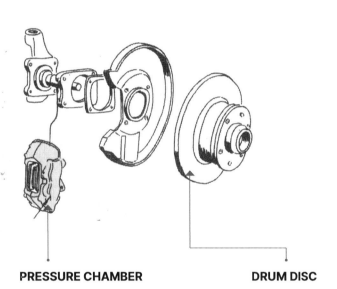

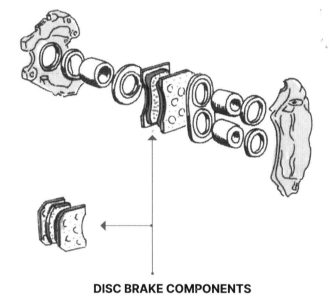

PRESSURE CHAMBER   **DRUM DISC**

DISC BRAKE COMPONENTS

To intensify braking, a depression power-assisted brake is used, achieving an effective and progressive braking on a smooth actuation of the brake pedal

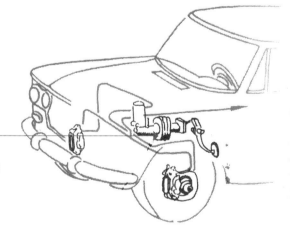

DEPRESSION POWER-ASSISTED BRAKE

15

THE WHEELS

They are the elements through which the vehicle moves

- ⌃ Allow to change **direction**
- ⌃ Sustain and **run** the vehicle in driving position
- ⌃ Achieve wheel drive
- ⌃ Allow **stopping** the vehicle
- ⌃ Absorb some of the small shocks due to road bumps

The vehicle wheels **have to be**

- ⌃ Resistant
- ⌃ Light
- ⌃ Correctly balanced.

Most passenger vehicles have 4 wheels, others less common, have 3 wheels

The number of wheels and – in some vehicles – their position influences the car stability:

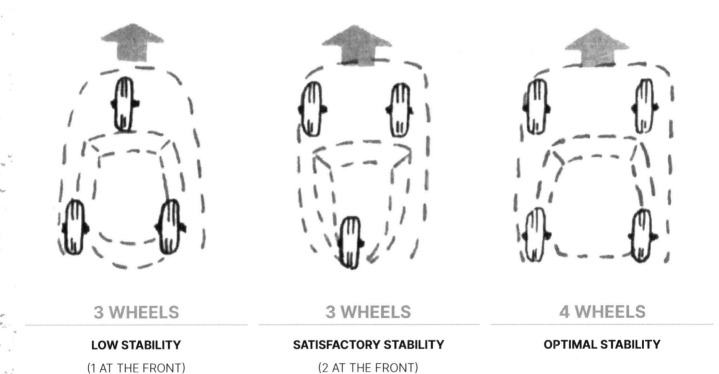

3 WHEELS	3 WHEELS	4 WHEELS
LOW STABILITY	**SATISFACTORY STABILITY**	**OPTIMAL STABILITY**
(1 AT THE FRONT)	(2 AT THE FRONT)	

The tyres represent the coating of the car wheels achieving a good adherence on the road and absorbing noises produced by the rolling of the wheels on the road

The air-cushions in the inner tubes become absorbers of the small shocks due to road bumps

THE WHEELS

The main parts of a wheel are the following:

The dimensions of the wheels are given in inches or milimeters (1 inch = 25.4 mm)

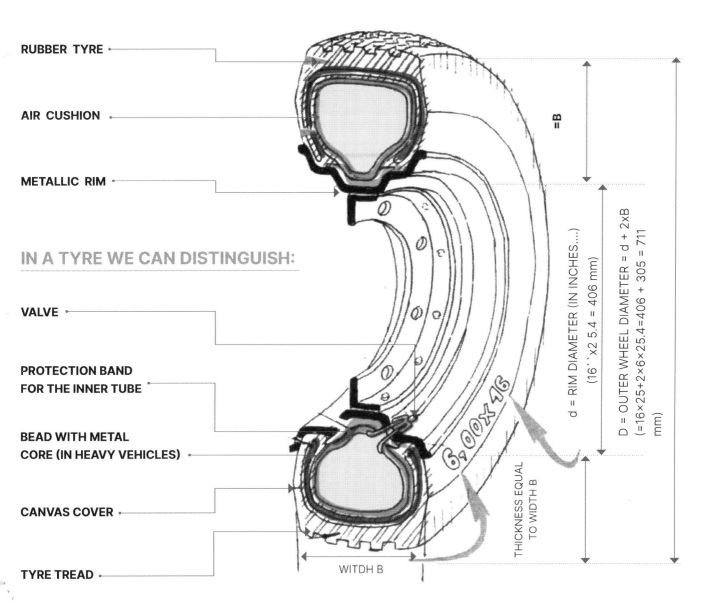

RUBBER TYRE

AIR CUSHION

METALLIC RIM

IN A TYRE WE CAN DISTINGUISH:

VALVE

PROTECTION BAND
FOR THE INNER TUBE

BEAD WITH METAL
CORE (IN HEAVY VEHICLES)

CANVAS COVER

TYRE TREAD

d = RIM DIAMETER (IN INCHES....)
(16'' x2 5.4 = 406 mm)

D = OUTER WHEEL DIAMETER = d + 2xB
(=16×25+2×6×25.4=406 + 305 = 711 mm)

= B

THICKNESS EQUAL TO WIDTH B

WITDH B

6,00x16

Tyres without inner tubes are used by certain modern vehicles. They have a soft rubber lining inside, which helps maintaining tightness with the rim. The hole made in the tyre when a sharp object (nail) penetrates is covered automatically by this soft rubber lining

These tyres ease cooling, but they also generate a significant decrease of air pressure while driving

16

THE VEHICLE BODY

Is the upper part of the vehicle assembled on a metallic frame, for the arrangement of the travel space

According to the construction of their body, cars bear various names, such as:

CONVERTIBLE CAR

With maxmum 8 seats, with completely open body, with flexible or retractable top

SEDAN

With 4...8 Seats, closed body and lateral windows

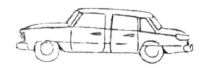

LIMOUSINE

With 4 up to 6 seats, closed body, 4 doors and separating window between the front and the back seats

CABRIOLET

With 2..4 Seats, with a 2-door body and flexible top (folding or retracting)

COUPÉ

With 2...3 Adjacent seats, closed 2-door body, and 2 or 4 door windows

COMMERCIAL VEHICLE
(OR AUTOSTATION)

For approximately 8 people or a load of 600 kgf, with closed body

THE VEHICLE BODY

Are made to achieve special performance:

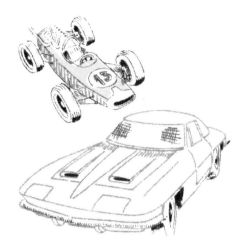

The race car is a performance construction with 1 or 2 seats and open body, meant to achieve speed performance

THE SPORTS CAR

Roadster – is a performance vehicle, usually having 2 seats, with open or closed body

SPECIAL VEHICLES

Are designed for specific usage, with additional equipment

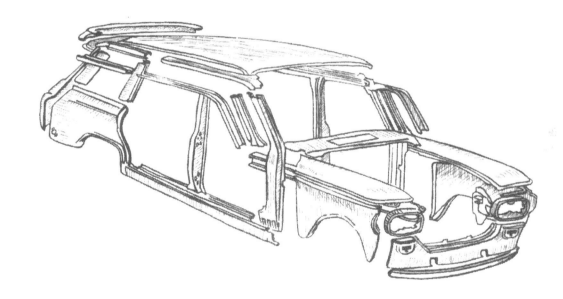

The body of a modern car is made of plates assembled by welding and screws and nuts .

The material used for this is steel sheet or plastic, seldom wood

17

THE ELECTRICAL SYSTEM

The electrical system of a car **is made of:**

- ⅄ A **power generator** that produces the power necessary to the vehicle;
- ⅄ A **battery**, that collects the electricity produced by the generator and sends it to the consumers when the generator is not working or when the voltage given by the generator is too low;
- ⅄ Various **consumers** such as: the ignition system, lighting system, optic and acoustic signalling, etc.
- ⅄ Controlling relays, signalling devices, conducting devices, etc.

A FEW DEFINITIONS

Voltage (u) is the difference in electric potential applied at an end in a circuit making an electric charge able to flow through the circuit

Resistance (r) is the property of materials to oppose to the flow of electric charge through them (4)

Electric current (i) is an electron oriented movement defined by the relation:

$$I = \frac{U}{R}$$

Power (p) in an electric circuit is defined as the product of the voltage and current flowing through the circuit:

$$P = U \times I$$

Units of measurement for the above physical quantities:

- ⅄ Voltage measured in volts (v);
- ⅄ Resistance measured in ohms (ω);
- ⅄ Current measured in ampers (a);
- ⅄ Power measured in watts (w)

THE DYNAMO

Is the power generator of a direct current used in cars and it operates based on the principle of electromagnetic induction`

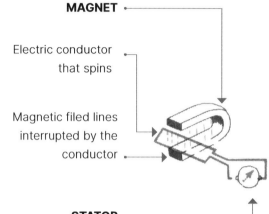

MAGNET

Electric conductor that spins

Magnetic filed lines interrupted by the conductor

If the magnetic field lines between the 2 poles n and s are interrupted by spinning an electric conductor closed at both ends, an induced electric current is created within the circuit

STATOR

The conductors are loop shaped and produce

Galvanometer (instrument that detects the electric current

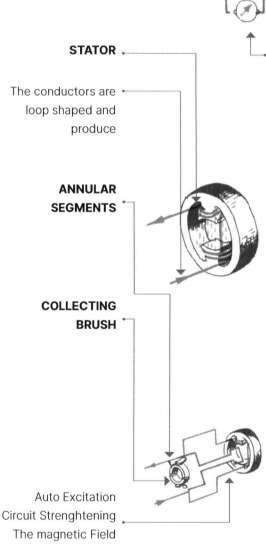

ANNULAR SEGMENTS

COLLECTING BRUSH

In the design of a dynamo, the magnetic field is created by the electromagnets forming the stator (or the inductor), which are powered from the generator terminals in parallel (derivation). This is called an auto-excitation circuit in derivation.

Alternating voltage. In order to redress it (to get a direct current) a collector with two brushes that collect current from two annular segments isolated from one another

Auto Excitation Circuit Strenghtening The magnetic Field

DYNAMO STUCTURE

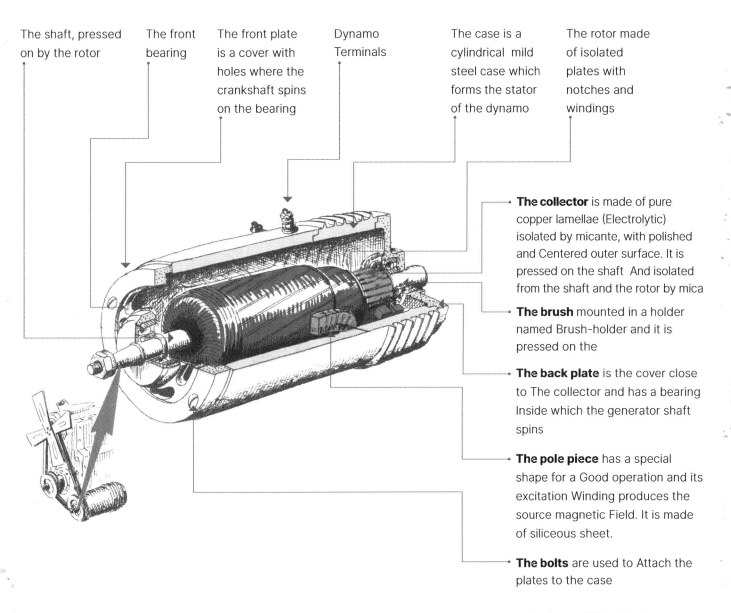

The shaft, pressed on by the rotor

The front bearing

The front plate is a cover with holes where the crankshaft spins on the bearing

Dynamo Terminals

The case is a cylindrical mild steel case which forms the stator of the dynamo

The rotor made of isolated plates with notches and windings

The collector is made of pure copper lamellae (Electrolytic) isolated by micante, with polished and Centered outer surface. It is pressed on the shaft And isolated from the shaft and the rotor by mica

The brush mounted in a holder named Brush-holder and it is pressed on the

The back plate is the cover close to The collector and has a bearing Inside which the generator shaft spins

The pole piece has a special shape for a Good operation and its excitation Winding produces the source magnetic Field. It is made of siliceous sheet.

The bolts are used to Attach the plates to the case

IMPORTANT FEATURES OF THE DIRECT CURRENT GENERATORS ON VEHICLES:

The dynamo shaft **is moved** by the engine crankshaft through a v belt. In most vehicles the same v belt moves both the dynamo and the water pump and also the cooling system fan getting over three pulleys (wheels for v belts)

The dynamo pulley has, in some vehicles, cooling fins that cool the dynamo

- ⅄ the nominal voltage that may be 6 or 12 v.
- ⅄ The voltage delivered by the dynamo terminals is actually higher, to be able to charge the car battery at 6.6v and 13.2v.
- ⅄ The nominal power measured in watts is 200-350w for cars, reaching 1000...1500 w for buses

The alternator or the alternating power generator replaces the dynamo in some vehicles, having the following advantages: light weight, reduced volume, ability to charge battery even at low dynamo speed, simple, robust structure, long life. It needs expensive rectifiers (germanium and silisium diodes). It is provided with only a voltage operated relay.

ALTERNATOR OPERATION

The alternator provides the electricity necessary for the operation of a vehicle.

When starting the car the battery is the one that provides the energy needed, whereupon the alternator goes into action. It charges the battery, providing the energy needed for all the electric and electronic components of the car.

The alternator has 3 (three) main components:

- Stator
- Rotor
- Diodes and voltage regulator

The alternator is actually an electric current generator. Its rotor is driven by the engine of the car through a transmission belt. By rotating the rotor, which is actually a magnet, an alternating induced voltage appears inside the stator.

The alternating voltage is transformed into constant voltage and stabilized with the help of diodes and voltage regulator.

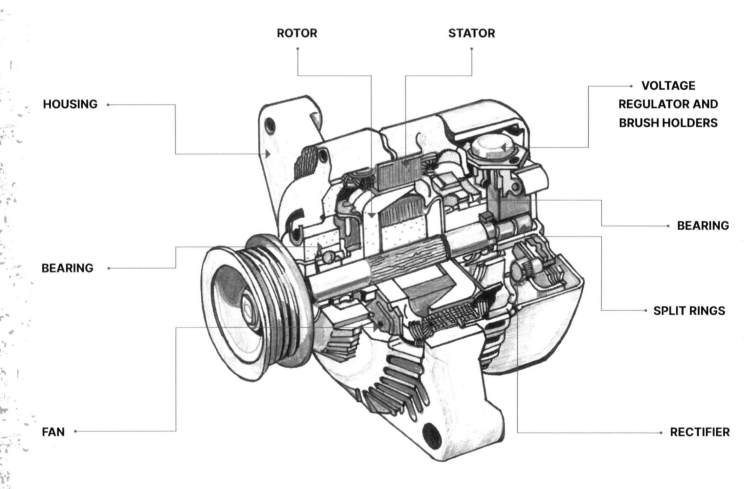

THE STARTER

Is an electrical engine powered by the battery that spins the crankshaft on starting the car engine

The structure of the starter is similar to that of the direct current generator (dynamo)

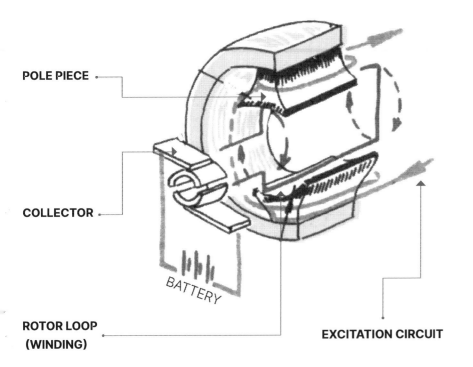

POLE PIECE

COLLECTOR

BATTERY

ROTOR LOOP
(WINDING)

EXCITATION CIRCUIT

The operation principle is based on electromagnetic induction.
A closed winding with a flowing current inside, situated in a magnetic field shall spin in a certain direction under the action of this field.
The electrical engine receives power and gives mechanical energy, while a dynamo receives mechanical energy and gives power

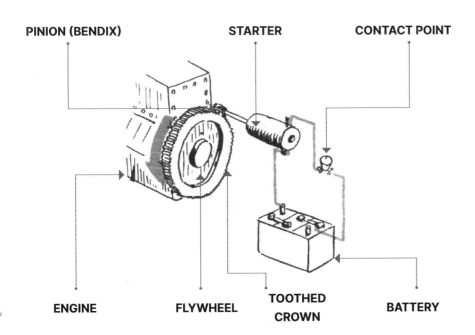

PINION (BENDIX)   STARTER   CONTACT POINT

ENGINE   FLYWHEEL   TOOTHED CROWN   BATTERY

Crankshaft spinning is done by the toothed crown on the engine flywheel.

The starter is fueled by the battery and the pinion on the starter shaft (named bendix) couples to the toothed crown on the flywheel, that it begins rotating, thus starting the engine.

A correct operation involves three stages of coupling the pinion (bendix) to the flywheel toothed crown

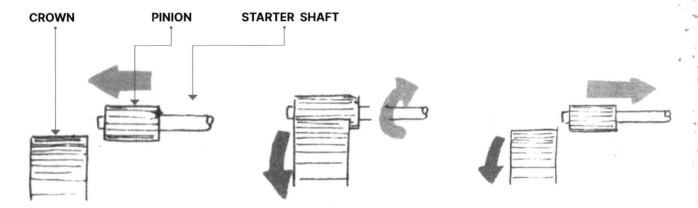

CROWN   **PINION**   **STARTER SHAFT**

Pinion helicoidal **forwarding** to allow its smooth coupling to the toothed crown on the flywheel

Spinning the pinion by coupling the starter to the battery and starting the car engine

Return and **stop** the pinion after starting the car engine

These stages are **achieved** by the structure and by the correct exploitation of the starting system.

The coupling mechanisms of the starter pinion may be:by inertia, mechanical, by electromagnet, etc., Allowing the movement of the pinion or even the starter rotor.

The **diagram** of a starter with **electromagnetic coupling** shows that by pressing the starter button, the pinion advances towards the crown and after they are engaged the starter couples to the battery, spinning the crankshaft.

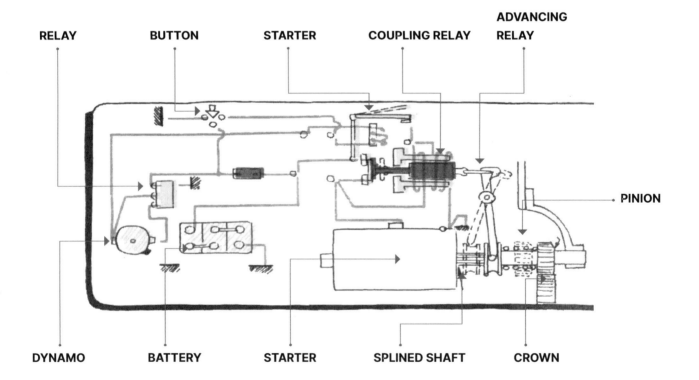

RELAY   **BUTTON**   **STARTER**   **COUPLING RELAY**   **ADVANCING RELAY**

PINION

DYNAMO   **BATTERY**   **STARTER**   **SPLINED SHAFT**   **CROWN**

AUTOMOTIVE BATTERY

It is a **tank of electrical power** received from the generator and given to the c onsumers:

- When the generator is not operating (the engine is stopped)
- When it operates at low speed (engine in idle mode)
- When it is overcharged (night driving)

The battery **operation** is based on certain chemical reactions produced inside it

Lead-acid batteries are generally used with cars and sometimes alkaline batteries, but rarely

The battery is made of 3 or 6 elements, each with voltage terminals of 2v

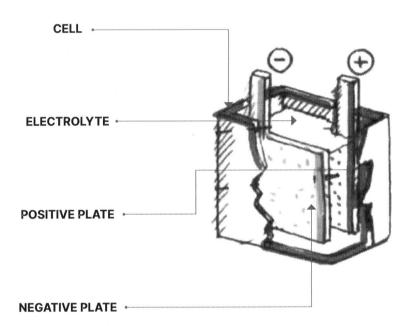

CELL

ELECTROLYTE

POSITIVE PLATE

NEGATIVE PLATE

ONE ELEMENT HAS:

- A positive plate made of lead dioxide (Pb_2)
- A negative plate made of spongy lead (Pb)
- A bakelite cell
- Electrolyte made of sulfuric acid Solution (H_2SO_4) dilluted in distilled water

Several elements connected serially or in parallel make up a car battery

The battery capacity (besides nominal voltage of 6 or 12 v) is an important feature. Measured in ampere hour and show how much energy it can provide until discharge. Batteries of 70...100 ah are used in cars, 150 ah (ampere hour) in trucks.

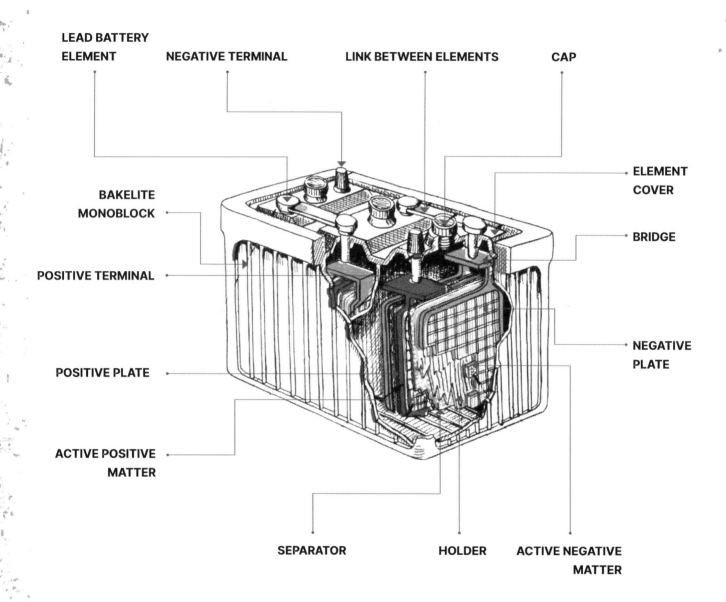

LEAD BATTERY ELEMENT

NEGATIVE TERMINAL

LINK BETWEEN ELEMENTS

CAP

ELEMENT COVER

BAKELITE MONOBLOCK

BRIDGE

POSITIVE TERMINAL

NEGATIVE PLATE

POSITIVE PLATE

ACTIVE POSITIVE MATTER

SEPARATOR

HOLDER

ACTIVE NEGATIVE MATTER

A normal operation of the car battery keeps a voltage level between 1.75 V and 2.7 V on every element, that is:

- In a 6 v battery, between 5.25 V and 8.1 V;
- In a 12 v battery, between 10.5 V and 18.2 V

The overload or the exaggerated discharge beyond the shown Limits, generate the battery destruction (sulphatation, loss of Capacity, fast discharge, etc.)

THE ELECTROCHEMICAL PROCESS

It is the basis of car battery

THE CAR BATTERY OPERATION HAS FOUR STAGES:

- Charged
- On discharge
- Discharged
- On charge.

CHARGED:

- There is lead dioxide
- (Pbo) at the positive plate 2
- There is spongy lead (pb)
- At the negative plate
- The electrolyte density
- Is 1.20...1.24 G/cm3 or 24°...28°Bé
- (Read bomé degrees)
- The voltage on terminals : 8 v (for 6 v batteries) and 16 v (for 12 v batteries)

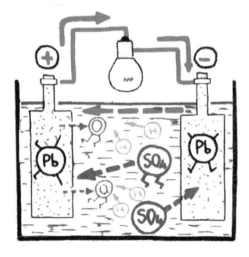

DISCHARGED:

- The lead sulfate (so pb) 4 has formed on both plates
- Electrolyte density decreased at approx. 1.12 G/cm3 or 16°bé
- Voltage (minimum allowed!) 5.25 V on a 6 v battery and 10.5 V on a 12 v battery

ON DISCHARGE :

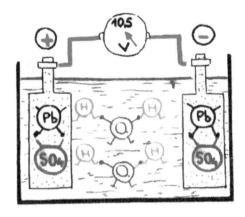

- ⅄ The oxygen **O** on the positive plate passes into the electrolyte and combines with the hydrogen H_2, forming water molecules H_2O
- ⅄ "The radical "SO_4 is deposited on the plates and here it combines with the lead **Pb** and the lead sulfate (SO_4Pb) is formed.
- ⅄ There is a decrease in the concentration of electrolyte by

ON CHARGE :

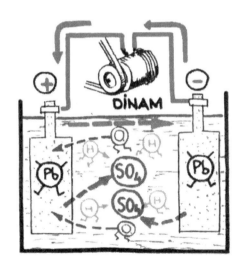

- ⅄ The lead sulfate (SO_4Pb) decomposes from both plates
- ⅄ SO_4Pb passses into the 4 electrolyte and combines with hydrogen h, forming sulfuric acid molecules (H_2SO_4)
- ⅄ Oxygen **O** combines with the lead pb on the positive plate forming lead dioxide (PbO_2)
- ⅄ Spongy lead **Pb** is left on the negatve plate
- ⅄ The electrolyte concentration increases at approx.1.22 gr/cm_3
- ⅄ Gases are released at the end of the charging process

The car battery is charged by the direct power generator (the dynamo) on the car, and at the garage it is done by a rectifier

RELAYS

The relay is an electromagnetic device used in order to protect the car electrical equipment

THE OPERATING PRINCIPLE OF A RELAY IS BASED ON ELECTROMAGNETISM:

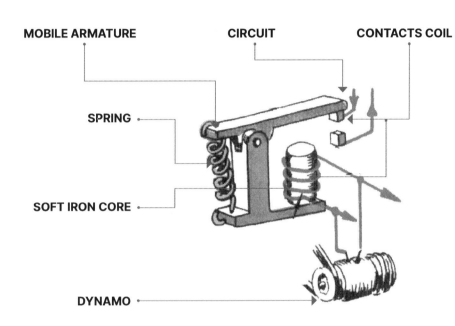

MOBILE ARMATURE   CIRCUIT   CONTACTS COIL

SPRING

SOFT IRON CORE

DYNAMO

At a certain dynamo speed, the Electric current flowing within **The coil** magnetizes **the soft iron Core**. It attracts **the mobile Armature** and **the contacts** close Forming an electric circuit; When the current given by the Dynamo weakens,**the spring** Becomes stronger than the Electromagnetic flow and Separates contacts that interrupt The wanted electric circuit

Relay blocks are used in cars, comprising usually three relays with The following functions:

RELAY	ENGINE SPEED	ACTION	EFFECT
1. Make and brake relay (reverse current relay)	Low	Breaks the circuit between the battery and dynamo	Avoids battery discharge on the dynamo when it has a lower voltage than the battery
	High	Closes the circuit between the battery and dynamo	Allows the battery to be charged by the dynamo when it has a higher voltage than the battery
2. Ballast	Normal	Brings resistance in to the autoexcitation dynamo circuit	Avoids damage to electric consumers caused by the excessive increase of voltage or the intensity of the current produced by the dynamo
3. Voltage regulator	Normal		

Diagram of a relay block (type rr-12)

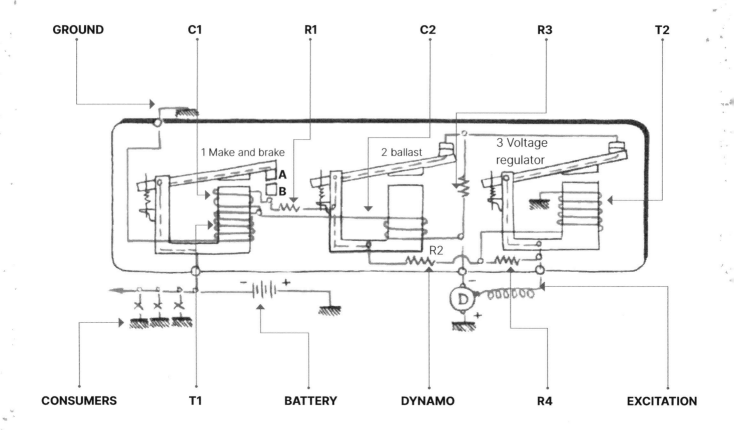

GROUND C1 R1 C2 R3 T2

1 Make and brake A B

2 ballast

3 Voltage regulator

R2

D

CONSUMERS T1 BATTERY DYNAMO R4 EXCITATION

In **operating** these relays, the following situations may occur:

1. **Too low dynamo speed (engine idle speed):**
   - The coil flow t fueled by the dynamo through coil c and frame is too low. The **A-B** contacts stay open
   - The Battery-Dynamo Circuit Is Broken, Avoiding Battery Discharge on the dynamo

2. **Normal dynamo speed reached:**
   - The T_1 coil flow increases, the electromagnetism attracts the mobile 1 Armature and closes the **A-B** contacts;
   - The dynamo charges the battery through the C_1 and C_2 coils , the A-B contacts and through the body of the make and brake relay

3. **Excessively increased dynamo speed**
   - Both voltage and intensity increase, endangering the operation of electric consumers;
   - The intensity coils C_2 and the voltage coils T_2 create flows attracting the armatures of relays 2 and 3 ;
   - In the dynamo excitation circuit resistances form and maintain voltage and intensity within limits allowed ;
   - The 2 voltage and intensity relays vibrate, being trigerred 50...100 times per second;

4. **Dynamo speed under the normal limit**
   - The A-B contacts stay closed and allow the battery to start discharging on the dynamo ;
     - The current flowing through c coil creates a reverse flow 1
     - Which rejects the armature and opens the a-b contacts discharging battery on the dynamo is avoided.

THE IGNITION SYSTEM

The car engine ignites the mixture through an electric spark produced by two electrodes of "the spark plug" in each cylinder the spark produced by the 6v or 12v battery cannot ignite the fuel and the compressed air mixture in the cylinder.

The mixture can be ignited by a **high voltage** spark (between 12000 v and 20000 v) produced by **the ignition system** that may be:

- By delco, fueled by the battery (used in most cars);
- By magneton, used mostly in motorcycles and less in cars

THE IGNITION SYSTEM FROM THE BATTERY IS MADE

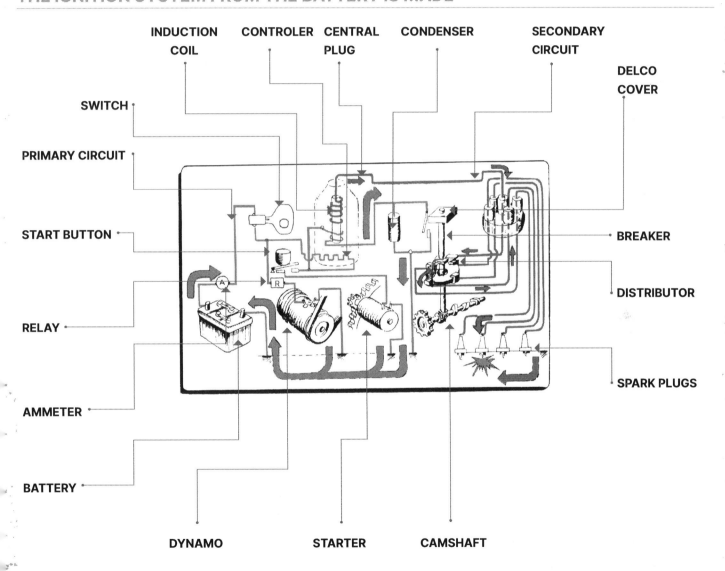

INDUCTION COIL   CONTROLER   CENTRAL PLUG   CONDENSER   SECONDARY CIRCUIT   DELCO COVER

SWITCH

PRIMARY CIRCUIT

START BUTTON

RELAY

AMMETER

BATTERY

BREAKER

DISTRIBUTOR

SPARK PLUGS

DYNAMO   STARTER   CAMSHAFT

Link through **the metallic frame** of the car

Its operation is based on the induction principle when in a low Voltage primary circuit (6 or 12 v and approx. 2...3 A) the current is Interrupted (interruption generated by the braker), in the secondary Coil a **high voltage** current (of 12,000...20,000 v and approx. 0.0005 A) is Generated.

This current flows through the **central plug**, is sent through the **distributor** to the **central electrode** of a **spark plug**. From here, the current jumps on the side electrode through a **high voltage spark**, able to ignite the fuel and the compressed air mixture

SPARK PLUG   **CYLINDER HEAD**

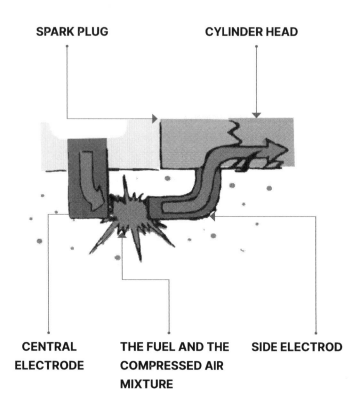

From the side electrode, the current returns through the cylinder head – engine – chassis (car frame) to the secondary coil where it started from, after going through a part of the secondary circuit, too.

CENTRAL   **THE FUEL AND THE**   **SIDE ELECTROD**
ELECTRODE   **COMPRESSED AIR**
                     MIXTURE

The induction coil plays the role of a transformer, having a primary coil with about 200 1mm wires and the secondary one with 15,000 0.1mm wires in diameter

The controller is a protection resistance that increases its value on high temperature due to high currents flowing. On starting the engine by the button the controller resistance is shorted out, allowing for stronger sparks to be produced, necessary particularly when the engine is cold.

The condenser is connected in parallel with the breaker. The sparks produced by the braker are absorbed by the condenser. In the absence of a condenser, the sparks produced in the braker make the high voltage in the secondary circuit decrease a lot and thus the spark produced by the spark plug cannot ignite the mixture.

THE SPARK PLUG

Is made of:

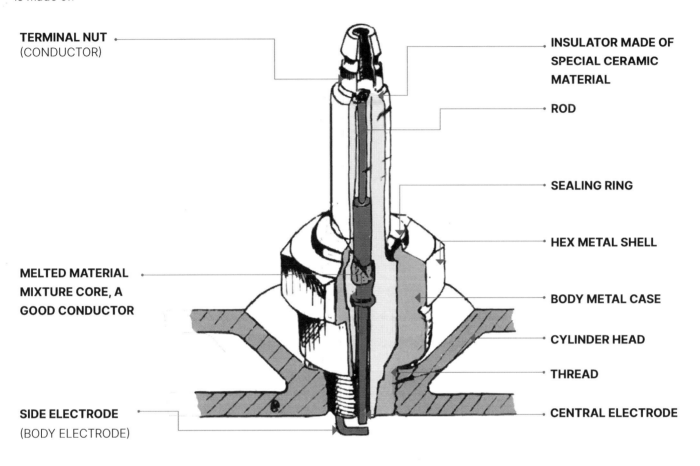

TERMINAL NUT
(CONDUCTOR)

**INSULATOR MADE OF
SPECIAL CERAMIC
MATERIAL**

ROD

SEALING RING

HEX METAL SHELL

**MELTED MATERIAL
MIXTURE CORE, A
GOOD CONDUCTOR**

BODY METAL CASE

CYLINDER HEAD

THREAD

SIDE ELECTRODE
(BODY ELECTRODE)

CENTRAL ELECTRODE

The length of the insulator lower part determines the heat elimination speed from the central electrode

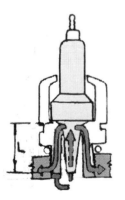

HOT SPARK PLUG

The heat in the Central
Electrode is Eliminated
Slowly, as it has a Long way
to go (The l lentgh of The
top is great)

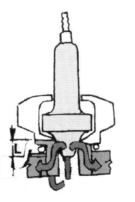

COLD SPARK PLUG

The heat in the central
electrode is eliminated fast,
as it has a short way to go
(the l lentgh of the top is
little).

The main features of a spark plug:

The **thread diameter** (spark plug dimension). The most widespread spark plugs have m14 (one should read: metric -14) or m18, that is the thread has the outer diameter of 14 or 18 mm.

The thermal transmittance is a number representing the spark plug rate of transfer of heat from the central electrode to the outside elements (cylinder cap, cooling water, etc).

A good choice of spark plug in terms of thermal transmittance is one that keeps the electrode top temperature between 500°c and 850°c

The spark plug temperature not within the limits has the following consequences:

Under 250°c	250-500⁰C	500° - 850°C selfcleaning temperature	850°C - 1200°C	Over 1200°c
Clogging in oil in fluid state	Clogging by carbonization of oil on the insulator	Selfcleaning operation	Premature ignitions uneven roll	Electrode and insulator melting
The spark plug is too cold (has a thermal transmittance value that is too big)	The spark plug Is suitable		The spark plug is too hot (has a thermal transmittance value that is too small)	

The thermal transmittance is exressed by a number that represents (for a great part of the european spark plugs) the time in seconds in which the spark plug reaches the preignition temperature, being mounted on a special engine. It results the following

- High thermal transmittance – many seconds – cold spark plug (225, 270, 310...)
- Medium thermal transmittance – suitable number of seconds – medium spark plug (145, 175...)
- Low thermal transmittance – few seconds – hot spark plug (25, 45, 75...)
- For other spark plugs the thermal transmittance represents the length Of the insulator top:
  - Long top = spark plug (hot spark plug)
  - Short top = spark plug (cold spark plug)

18

INDICATORS

The ammeter shows the intensity of the charge and discharge current of the battery

It is made of a horseshoe magnet or a bar magnet comprising:

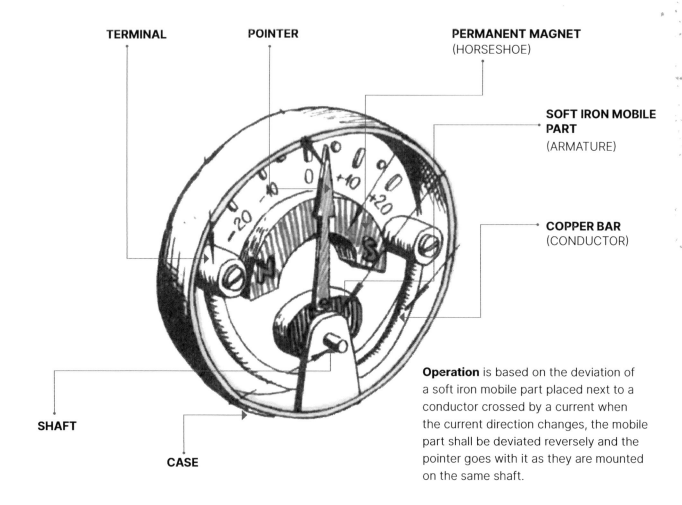

TERMINAL POINTER PERMANENT MAGNET (HORSESHOE)

SOFT IRON MOBILE PART (ARMATURE)

COPPER BAR (CONDUCTOR)

SHAFT

CASE

Operation is based on the deviation of a soft iron mobile part placed next to a conductor crossed by a current when the current direction changes, the mobile part shall be deviated reversely and the pointer goes with it as they are mounted on the same shaft.

When the device is in idle state (no current flows through the conductor), the pointer is in the middle showing "zero" and the mobile armature is in balance, determined by the permanent magnetic field.

The negative values (to the left) on the indicator show that battery is discharging

The positive values (to the right)on the indicator show that battery is charging with the current from the dynamo

The precision of ammeters used on cars is low, and the scale is divided from 5 to 5 or from 10 to 10 amperes

They are used for :

- Electric current
- (Ammeter)
- Fuel (fuel gauge)
- Water temperature
- (Thermometer)
- Oil pressure (manometer)

The fuel gauge shows the amount of fuel in the tank and it is made of a transmitter mounted on the tank and a receiver set on the dashboard, with the following components:

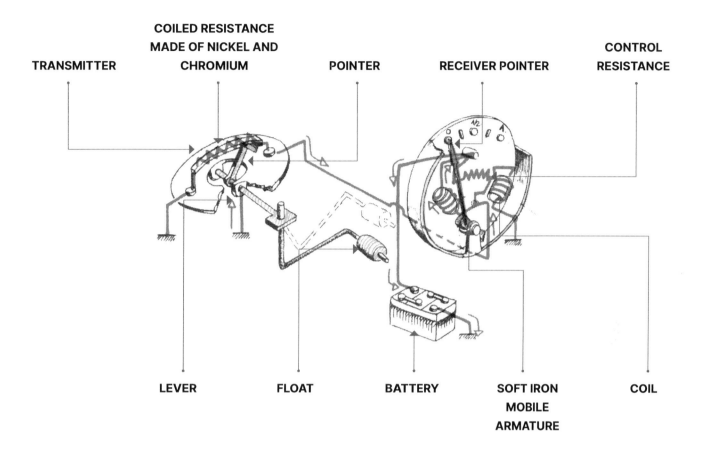

The following situations may occur in the gauge **operation**:

When the tank is **empty**, the float is down and the transmitter coiled resistance is taken Out of the circuit, so that the coil to the left receives a maximum current on the Marked circuit. Its flow attracts the mobile armature and the pointer shows "zero".

When the tank is full, the float raises and the coil to the left of the receiver will get a Weaker current as the coiled transmitter resistance interferes into the circuit. The Mobile armature shall be attracted by the coil to the right too, so that the pointer Indicates 1 (full).

For intermediate positions of the float, the pointer shall indicate ¼ , ½ or ¾, according to the amount of fuel in the tank. The receiver resistance is used to calibrate the fuel gauge

The thermometer indicates the temperature of water in the Cooling system; it is made of a transmitter placed into the Cooling water and a receiver placed on the dashboard:

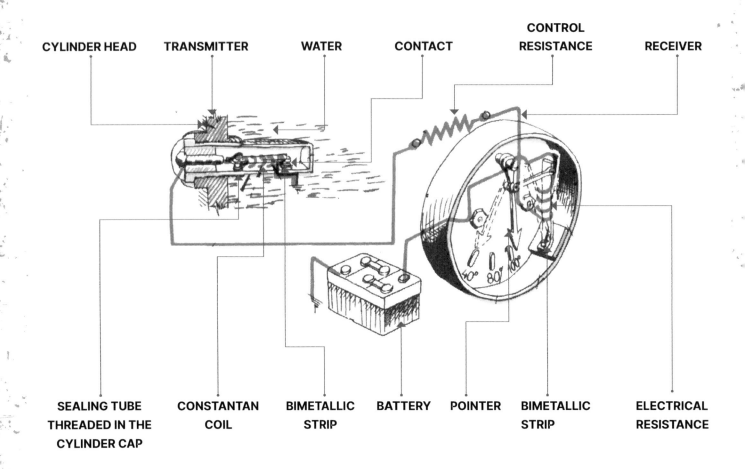

CYLINDER HEAD   TRANSMITTER   WATER   CONTACT   CONTROL RESISTANCE   RECEIVER

SEALING TUBE THREADED IN THE CYLINDER CAP   CONSTANTAN COIL   BIMETALLIC STRIP   BATTERY   POINTER   BIMETALLIC STRIP   ELECTRICAL RESISTANCE

It operates based on breaking a circuit due to the bending of a Metallic strip (made of two metals with different expansion Coefficients) when the current crosses an electrical Resistance.

When water has a **low temperature,** the environment being Colder a longer time is needed to warm the transmitter Bimetallic strip, its bending and circuit braking. As the curent Flows from the battery through both bimetallic strips for a Longer time, the receiver strip becomes hot and its bending Shall make the pointer show a low temperature (close to 40°c).

When water has a **high temperature**, the transmitter Bimetallic strip shall become hot faster and brake the Circuit that feeds the two strips. Contacts will be closed for A shorter time and the receive strip shall bend less, the Pointer showing a higher temperature (close to 100°c)

The manometer indicates the oil pressure in the Engine lubrication system ; it is made of a transmitter Connected to an oil pipe and a receiver:

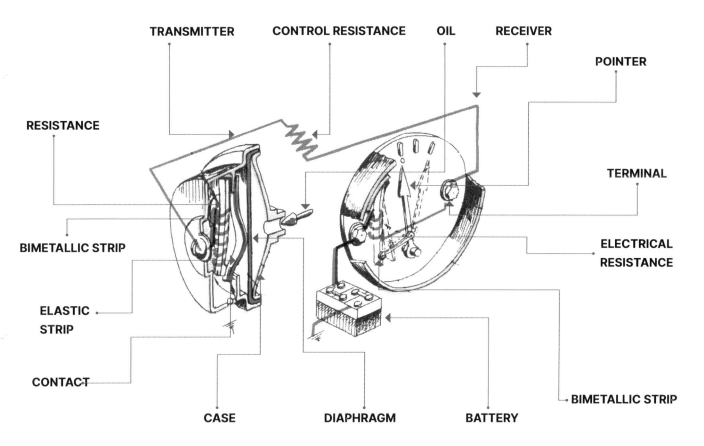

It functions – the same as the thermometer – based on the bending of the Bimetallic strips when they are heated

If there is **no oil pressure**, the current feeds both bimetallic strips. The Receiver strip bends a little and the pointer indicates "zero". The transmitter Strip brakes contacts by bending, and the battery current does not feed the Strips. The transmitter strips becomes cold, straightens closing the contacts And everything repeats. The receiver pointes does not oscillate, having a higher Thermal inertia.

When oil pressure occurs, it is transmitted to the diaphragm, pressing the Elastic strip that forces the contacts to break when the bimetallic strip Receives more heat. In the receiver, the heating of the bimetallic strip makes it Bend more, pushing the pointer to show a higher pressure.

19

SIGNALS

The following are used on cars:

- Optical signals (direction)
- Acoustic signals (horn)

The horn is an acoustic signal made of:

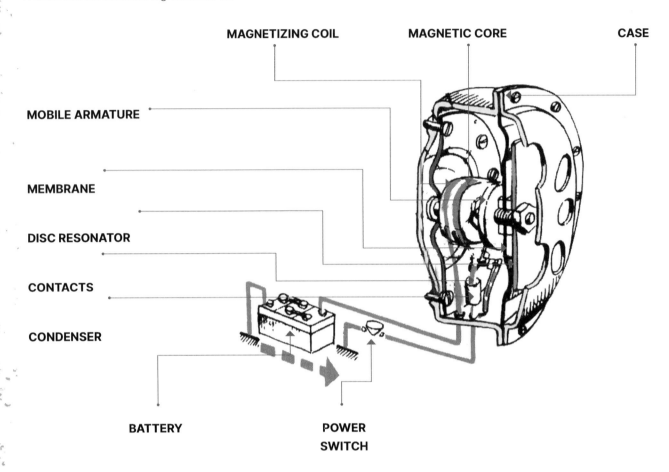

The horn **functions** based on the **electromagnetic** principle: when the current flows through the magnetizing coil, the magnetic core is magnetized, attracts the mobile armature which breaks the two contacts. The current cannot feed the coil anymore and the armature comes back, closing again the contacts and it all repeats, producing the membrane vibration.

The condenser is meant to eliminate sparks made by the repeated closure of contacts.

The electromagnetic horn **wear** is low, and **the sound** may be heard From up 150 m.

Sound is **amplified** by mounting resonant funnels in such a position that their length is half the wavelength of the basic membrane vibrations

The pleasant tones appear by two or three horns tuned and simultaneously actuated by a relay

The electropneumatic horns have a more pleasant sound, but they are more expensive, being actuated by an electrical engine that moves an air compressor, having a membrane and a funnel

The turn signal used by vehicles has intermittent light, being made from bimetal or hot thread

A turn signal with bimetal is made of:

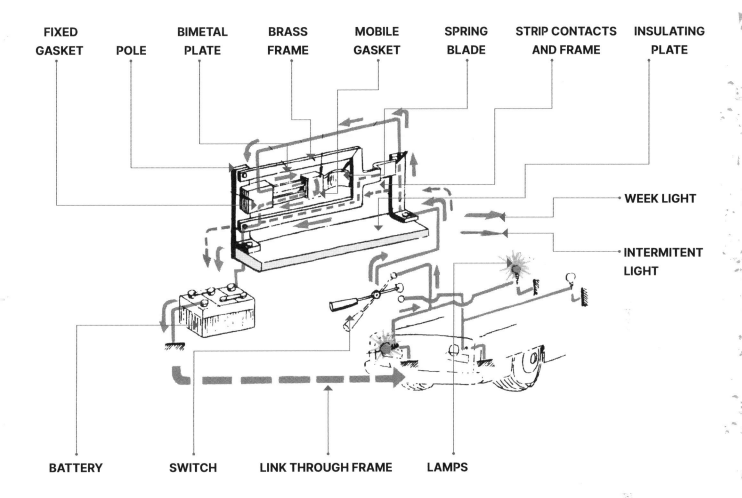

FIXED GASKET

POLE

BIMETAL PLATE

BRASS FRAME

MOBILE GASKET

SPRING BLADE

STRIP CONTACTS AND FRAME

INSULATING PLATE

WEEK LIGHT

INTERMITENT LIGHT

BATTERY

SWITCH

LINK THROUGH FRAME

LAMPS

It operates based on the bimetallic plate property to bend when heated (as the two metals have different expansion coefficients). When the switch is coupled, the current flows through the bimetal plate that has a high resistance, producing a weak light of lamps. The bimetallic plate bends when heated, bending also the brass frame, which makes contact with the right pole, shortcircuiting the bimetal (that will cool) feeding the lamps in normal flow. The phenomenon is repeated and the lamps have intermittent light.

20

HEADLIGHTS AND LAMPS

The headlights allow the vehicle to roll during night time having two compulsory lighting possibilities:

- ⋏ Distant lighting (or high beam)
- ⋏ Close lighting (or low beam)

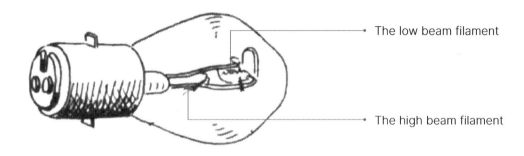

The low beam filament

The high beam filament

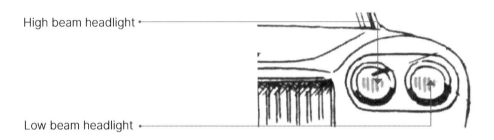

High beam headlight

Low beam headlight

Biphase lights ("bilux") are frequently used in headlights having two filaments and three contacts: -one filament for the high beam, located in the optical centre of the headlight -one filament for the low beam, located outside the optical centre of the headlight, being screened in front and down positions and allowing the light beam to light the upper part, towards the edge of the headlight

Some cars have four headlights, two inner ones (for the high beam) and two outer ones (for the low beam)

The operation **voltage** for lamps is 6.75 V in vehicles with 6 v electrical system and 13.5 V in vehicles with 12 v electrical system, determining a lifetime of 75 hours for the high intensity lamps and 300 hours for the low intensity lamps. This is approximately a quarter of the life of a fixed operation lamp (without mechanical vibrations).

The headlight reflector is u-shaped in order to achieve a maximum lighting. It may be covered with:

- ⋏ Aluminum (maximum lighting, frequently used)
- ⋏ Silver (good lighting but oxidizes easily)
- ⋏ By nickel cladding (diminished lighting and expensive to make)
- ⋏ By chromium cladding (good lighting, resistant and quite cheap)

The low beam may be **symmetrical** or **asymmetrical**:

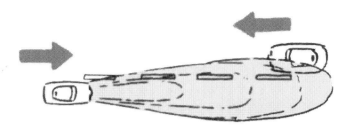 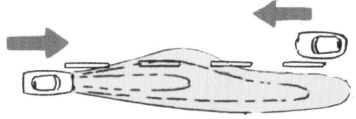

SYMMETRICAL LIGHTING

Small lighting distance(reducing speed is necessary) and in small deviations it blinds the oncoming vehicle. It is not used anymore

ASYMMETRICAL LIGHTING

On the right side the lighting distance is greater (allows going on high speed), avoiding to blind the oncoming vehicle. It is currently being used.

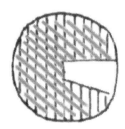

Asymmetrical lighting is achieved by using lamps with asymmetrical filament and special light dispersers (headlight glass) with an asymmetrical gap.

The modern car headlight is adjustable. The yellow headlights are used for fog, as the yellow light has a longer wavelength, that penetrates fog deeper and easier, eliminating the self-blinding phenomenon. When the water drops are big (wet fog) the yellow light has a reduced effect.

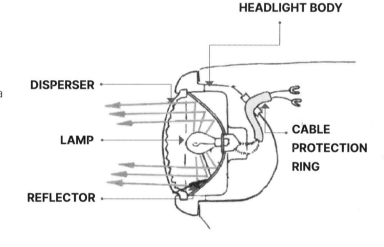

HEADLIGHT BODY

DISPERSER

LAMP

REFLECTOR

CABLE PROTECTION RING

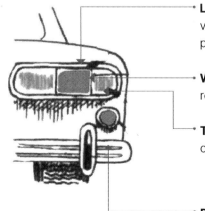

Lamps - The modern vehicles have multiple functions: signalling when vehicle is stopped (stop), engaged mechanically, hydraulically or pneumatically, once the brake pedal is pressed;

White signal (lighting) for reverse, engaged by the gearbox controlling rod;

Turning signal, with intermittent lighting, engaged by a special contractor;

Parking lights

Printed in Great Britain
by Amazon

13948363R00068